DRESSAGE FOR
NO COUNTRY

Also by Paul Belasik

Nature, Nurture and Horses

The Essential Paul Belasik

A Search for Collection: Science and Art in Riding

*Exploring Dressage Technique: Journeys into the
Art of Classical Riding*

*Riding Towards the Light: An Apprenticeship
in the Art of Dressage Riding*

*The Songs of Horses: Seven Stories for
Riding Teachers and Students*

Dressage for the 21st Century

DRESSAGE FOR
NO COUNTRY

Paul Belasik

TRAFALGAR SQUARE
North Pomfret, Vermont

First published in 2019 by
Trafalgar Square Books
North Pomfret, Vermont 05053

Disclaimer of Liability
The author and publisher shall have neither liability nor responsibility to any person or entity with respect to any loss or damage caused or alleged to be caused directly or indirectly by the information contained in this book. While the book is as accurate as the author can make it, there may be errors, omissions, and inaccuracies.

Trafalgar Square Books encourages the use of approved safety helmets in all equestrian sports and activities.

Library of Congress Cataloging-in-Publication Data
Names: Belasik, Paul, author.
Title: Dressage for no country / Paul Belasik.
Description: North Pomfret, Vermont : Trafalgar Square Books, 2019. |
  Includes index.
Identifiers: LCCN 2018037119 | ISBN 9781570769146 | ISBN 9781570769443 (ebook)
Subjects: LCSH: Belasik, Paul. | Dressage horse trainers--Biography. |
  Dressage.
Classification: LCC SF309.482.B45 A3 2019 | DDC 798.2/3--dc23
LC record available at https://lccn.loc.gov/2018037119

Book design by Lauryl Eddlemon
Cover design by RM Didier
Cover illustration by Elise Genest
Index by Michelle Guiliano, LinebyLineIndexing.com
Typeface: Palatino
Printed in the United States of America

10 9 8 7 6 5 4 3 2 1

To all the people who teach riding.

Contents

Acknowledgments

I would like to thank Martha Cook, Managing Director at Trafalgar Square Books, for her encouragement and advice over the years that have gone beyond this book, and Rebecca Didier for her hard work on not just her thoughtful edits but on the look of the whole project. Thank you also to Caroline Robbins, Publisher. Thanks to my wife Rose for countless hours, helping me repair the manuscript and her valuable feedback as another writer. Thanks to Lauryl Eddlemon for her design work and to Elise Genest for her beautiful painting on the book's cover.

INTRODUCTION

I WAS IN THE AIRPORT IN AMSTERDAM. It was the middle of the night. All the shops were closed. My eyes were burning, my skin was buzzing. If I could only get some sleep.

I made my way to the gate for my connecting flight. It was a small gate with maybe a dozen hard, plastic, tulip-shaped chairs anchored into the white tile floor that continued down the seemingly endless hall. I knew I had a couple hours' wait. There were four or five other people scattered around. I tried to make myself comfortable, to close my eyes. Some part of me was afraid I would fall fast asleep and miss the boarding call, perhaps find myself stranded, so I struggled with myself.

My gate was separated from the next by a wall of glass; it felt like I was looking into a big, empty fish tank. The lights on the other side were dim, and there were rows and rows of the same hard chairs, the same white floor. Something in the sterile scene caught my attention, some movement. A dark object was skittering along the colorless ground. I looked more closely. It was a mouse. In zigs and zags it worked its way under the seats and out again, across the room. Looking for what? Some forgotten crumb from the last passengers, some morsel of reward. As I watched his methodical searching, I wondered where he could possibly live in such a harsh environment, where his family was, how they came to be there... and *why?*

Even in my dazed state, the metaphor did not escape me. *I was that mouse.* In the middle of the night, in some inhospitable environment, searching. I had been in this psychological and physical place many times. *Why?*

You see, I come from a country with no tradition or history of dressage. Dressage, the training of horses with roots that go back to the ancient Greek philosopher and soldier Xenophon 2,000 years ago, has strong similarities to human ballet. Dressage reached one of its highest pinnacles in northern Italy in the 1500s. There, at the riding school of Giovanni Battista Pignatelli, young noblemen came from all over Europe to study this kind of riding. They returned to their own countries of France, Germany, Spain, and England, and although certain nationalistic elements shaded their riding in the centuries that followed, in reality, all the styles were similar. They all came from the same spring of knowledge. This dressage was an art form and discipline. It was an ethical way to train horses and the people who rode and worked with them. It also became one of the most sophisticated experiments in cross-species communication that the world has ever known.

If you want to truly understand this equestrian pursuit as an American, you are in a predicament—*especially* when you don't have much money. It is a life of travel to generally rural, not well-known places. You have to gain entry to other cultures as you seek the epicenter of the discipline and access to those who have mastered it and who might teach it to you. Your own history is not important. On the other hand, trapped by no national culture, your ignorance is a gift. Nothing is in your mind—the Zen mirror is clean. You have nothing to uphold, no country, no family, no school to defend. You are free.

Free to do what? To go where? To learn? But from whom? Like the mouse in the empty airport, all you can do is set out and start the search.

This book is about a lifetime of searching and studying. On the pages ahead I will illustrate some of the dressage systems I have studied. I have tried to be ruthlessly honest in talking about the deep problems these systems may have presented to me and to others. In the end, I talk about what the future of this art form might look like and how science has always been a partner to its continued development.

1

THE 1970s:
THE PLANES
COME WEST

German Horses and the
German System

"EUGEN WAHLER IS COMING!"

Everyone was excited. The small group of Trakehner breeders was expecting a visit from, if not the pope, then certainly a cardinal of the German horse breeding establishment. Eugen Wahler was one of only a few civilians outside the German government to be allowed to conduct the testing of young stallions for the state, determining which ones would be allowed as breeding stock. He was also a respected breeder at his own farm Klosterhof Medingen.

I, too, was excited, because it looked like I would be able to get a few riding lessons from this icon. (To give the reader some idea of the importance and the longevity of influence of Wahler, some forty years later, in 2012, 2013, and 2015, 2016, and 2017, the top German dressage stallion De Niro stood at Klosterhof Medingen.)

Discovering the German System

I had moved my horse operation from southern Pennsylvania to northern New York in the 1970s, and through a series of coincidences, began to train horses and stand stallions for the Trakehner Farm Burenhof—a small but growing breeding farm owned by Fritz and Roswitha Daemen-Van Buren. Fritz was one of the funniest people I had ever met. He and his wife were extremely supportive of my riding and training, and we became good friends. The couple was part of a serious group of Trakehner enthusiasts who became the founders of the American Trakehner Association. They aimed to imitate the German system in North America, with the goal of producing quality performance horses on US soil.

The German paradigm was, at this point, already influencing North American dressage. Even before I left Pennsylvania, many European riders and trainers (who seemed enthralled with America) regularly visited and taught in the States. Fritz Stecken, one of the brothers in a powerful German equestrian family, actually lived in Pennsylvania, only a few miles from my stable. The European presence impacted the American dressage experience not only with the style of teaching but with the automatic preference and promotion of the horses that riders and trainers from the Continent were already used to. These were Warmblood horses primarily descended from those bred in East Prussia to be versatile cavalry mounts. The modern German breeding systems evolved out of these initial requirements: horses began to be selected and tested for dressage ability, cross-country jumping, some speed elements, and stadium jumping, as well. For a young trainer like me, who had his start in the sport of eventing (which involved all these disciplines), the training system for the young German horses was a natural fit. It was everything I was already doing. So, with the lead of the Daemens, I went for full immersion in German methodology and culture, embracing the rare opportunity to train, show, and stand horses of a quality and scope I could never have afforded on my own.

On one weekend, I rode three fantastic stallions at home; Sue and Terry Williams let me sit on the now legendary Abdullah, who went on to win gold and silver medals at the 1984 Olympics in show jumping; and Henry Schurink of Doornhof Farm in Vermont—who imported the first Trakehner stallion to the States in 1961—let me ride Romelos and Hexenmeister. (Romelos, a big powerful horse, was owned by the Daemens, and Hexenmeister would be the future sire of a young horse I went on to train to FEI levels.) I think I was riding as many German horses as anyone in America.

Today, if one speaks about the "German system," it is likely to involve the Classical Training Scale, consisting of six principles, often depicted in a pyramid shape, implying ascension from one phase to the next. This pyramid is an overly simplistic graphic; the German system that I studied and learned was not perfectly clear, nor was it simple. Some of its strongest messages and best advice were below the surface.

The system I learned had several key elements. The first might seem obvious: young horses were started and ridden more for versatility, in the style of eventing. They had to be round and on the bit, capable of dressage movements, but not at a very high level, as they were immature in body and mind. The early training in preparation for jumping was probably more important, especially from an economic point of view, since prices for jumpers at the top of their field dwarfed prices for dressage horses at the top of theirs. When a horse did specialize in dressage, *The*

Principles of Riding: The Official Instruction Handbook of the German National Equestrian Federation gave the following advice under "further training for the specialist horse," plainly stating, "All these high school [airs above the ground] are very rarely executed and only by especially suitable horses. It is therefore unnecessary to provide further explanation." It was clear that training ended at piaffe, passage, and pirouettes, that we were not to pursue movements where both of the horse's front legs would come off the ground at once. The horses were to be ridden athletically *forward*.

The versatile young horse was trained by an equally versatile rider who, for the most part, rode in a balanced seat—not just the typical forward seat. The horse was often big and strong, and because he was ridden in a snaffle, he might take considerable contact in the bridle. He could tend to have a stiff, bouncy trot, and be a more physical ride than the Thoroughbreds I and other American riders were used to. The German horse was longed in side-reins, and even at a minimal level, worked in-hand in preparation for being exhibited at performance testings and breed shows.

A Rectangular Shape

In general, I don't think the average person would have been able to see much difference between the training of German horses and of young horses from other European countries. However, there were secondary requirements of these German horses that dictated and shaped the riding style. These were less obvious, but no less important.

The great Dr. Fritz Schilke, a father figure in the German breeding scene (particularly Trakehners, in his case), insisted that horses be bred for conformation that fit a rectangular frame, as opposed to the squarer frame of the Thoroughbred or Iberian horses. I'm certain that, at least in some part, this came out of a carriage-driving heritage where the Warmblood horse was admired for a "floating" trot. In fact, this breeding model has not significantly changed in philosophy. The Director of the Hanoverian *Verband* (Association) as of writing, Dr. Werner Schade, was noted in *The Horse Magazine's* article, "What Made German Dressage Great," as saying, "The formation of the neck, the shoulder, the saddle position, the topline, the hind end construction, the uphill construction, and the rectangular frame are some of the most important conformation criteria."

When Eugen Wahler finally did come to the United States, I could see his job was to acknowledge the effort of the North America pioneer breeders. You could feel the heavy importance of his validation for some of them. They had invested a lot more than just money. (I rode a horse or two for him—he was gracious, but above all a horseman through and through.)

Over the years, though, as I rode and studied the art of equitation, I began to find problems with this rule of conformation in that these "long" horses were more difficult to collect. It was early on that I began a lifelong habit of measuring the length of a horse's back, finding a direct correlation between that length and his ability to collect. (Or, at least, a connection between the length of the back and *not* being able to collect.) When I say "collect," I mean in the most simple terms that the horse would use his lumbar-pelvic muscles the *iliopsoas* and *psoas*, among others, to "curl" his hindquarters under, so that if you drew a line from the point of the buttocks to the ground, the hocks would be in front of the line and not buried in the hair of the tail (behind the line). Even when a horse shows marked flexion in his hocks, stifles, and hind legs, and lowers his hindquarters, he is not necessarily demonstrating "classic collection" if his hips do not come under his body in the way I've described.

The notion of "true collection" is a simple and ancient one, which came from the fact that the old dressage masters loved the *airs above the ground*—the series of high level, classical dressage movements in which the horse leaves the ground. For a horse to raise his front end off the ground, he had to rebalance his weight toward the rear, widen his stance, and bring his hind legs under his mass, like a weightlifter getting under the weight to be lifted. It was simple physics. Even if a rider did not aspire to airs above the ground, lightening the horse's forehand and rebalancing him toward the rear became the *raison d'être* of dressage. William Cavendish, Duke of Newcastle and author of *A General System of Horsemanship*, said, "The whole object of the school horse was to get the horse upon the haunches." However, when German officials dismissed the airs above the ground as too rare, too specialized, and unnecessary to explain, capping dressage training at a level below them, they accidentally opened the door to a lot of confusion about the true end goal of classical dressage. Coupled with a long-backed horse bred for his gaits rather than his ability to collect, a certain outcome became inevitable.

In an interview with Dr. Schade, Chris Hector, editor of *The Horse Magazine*, asked why:

I asked [Dr. Schade] why it seemed easier to produce jumping stallions than dressage stallions... [Dr. Schade replied], "This is a very interesting question. For me there are three reasons: firstly the qualities a jumping horse requires have a higher level of heritability in comparison to the dressage traits. The number and variety of qualities a dressage horse requires is higher than the number of qualities that a jumping horse requires. And thirdly, the training way to the international top class is more difficult for dressage horses and with a stronger dependence on the competence of the riders. Therefore it is easier for a jumping stallion to come through in the breed."

I think Werner Schade's hypothesis has merit. However, I feel it does not address the possibility that the long-standing allegiance to breeding German horses with a rectangular frame may not be producing horses that can collect more easily, and furthermore, that collection should not be overlooked as the heart and soul of dressage.

A Commercial Mandate

Another important aspect of the German system is revealed in Dr. Fritz Schilke's pointed advice to breeders and trainers, which went something like this: No breed ever died from lack of type; breeds die from lack of marketability.

Early on in my career, I got this message. This kind of directive from owners, breeders, and bosses had as much to do with how a rider rides and a trainer trains as do lessons on position or technique. There is business to be done, stallions to be booked, young horses made ready to be sold. One had a limited amount of time to make an impression with a horse, so one had better make it good! If one rode in competitions, win. If one showed sale horses, impress the observer. This fostered a short-term mentality and encouraged flamboyancy over correctness. The bottom line (no pun intended) was a commercial mandate, not a stylistic or artistic one. The drive to win was not the simple aspect of pure sport, with individuals aspiring to high achievement; it was part of a wider, far-reaching, pragmatic sales industry. If it is important to win competitions to promote one's horses, one will need to get into positions of power on rules committees and judges' training programs. One needs to dominate publicity and press however one can.

This promotion of the Warmblood has a long history. The German chief equerry and mastermind of the German breeding program, Dr. Gustav Rau, tried to eliminate the Lipizzaner from the Spanish Riding School in Vienna, Austria. Alois Podhajsky, long-time Director of the Spanish Riding School, said Rau told him in all seriousness, "If you succeed in building up the art of classic horsemanship with Hanoverian horses at the Spanish Riding School, your reputation will be made." In the book *The International Warmblood Horse: A Worldwide Guide to Breeding and Bloodlines* by Celia Clarke and Debbie Wallin, Dr. Hanfried Haring, the Managing Director of the Breeding Department of the German Equestrian Federation and Managing Director of the German Olympic Committee, says in the first paragraph of his foreword, "In the last decade, the Warmblood has triumphed round the world as a sport horse. It has ousted other breeds, which were the traditional winners in the three Olympic equestrian disciplines." The tone is inescapable, and if it echoes the late Gustav Rau's remarks to Alois Podhajsky that his reputation would somehow be lacking if he did not use Hanoverians in the Spanish Riding School, it is because it is virtually identical in sentiment. Other breeds, according to Haring, were "ousted." There is an active inference of the superiority of Warmbloods.

At the least, one can appreciate the 50 years of consistent and aggressive promotion of their horses by the German breeding authorities. Breeders and businesses provided horses for up-and-coming American riders to compete; in exchange, when the horses sold, riders received commissions and boosts to their own careers. To this day, one can argue about which nation has produced the best dressage, but you cannot argue about which nation is the best at the *business* of dressage.

A Scientific Approach

The German breeding and training system relied heavily on a penchant for metrics. Everything was measured, data collected. The theory was that a scientific approach would be applied to make the horses better and better. As I was learning the German system in its intricacies, and even benefitting from its strengths by being able to show horses of a higher quality and of the sort that judges were becoming enamored with, I was also beginning to see some drawbacks. When it came to the selection of stallions, it was pretty much a government-regulated activity. Stallions were tested and approved at approximately three years old; those unapproved were not allowed to be used for breeding, at least in Germany. I asked, where was the data to support the decision that breeding horses in this way worked? That there was more causation, not just correlation between phenotype, a horse's own physical make-up and his genotype, the genetic potential he might possess and may or may not pass on? In other countries, breeding programs were vastly different. Under German rules, the Canadian-bred Northern Dancer, an extremely important sire in Thoroughbred racehorses, would never have been allowed to breed because he was too small and the wrong "type." A horse like Milton, a British Sport Horse and one of the greatest show jumpers ever, would never have been born because his sire Maurius would not have been approved in Germany (he was in Holland). One had to wonder what genetic gold was rejected because of rules about the physical body that contained it.

This is where marketability would come in: a demand can be manufactured. Sometimes, the demand theory cannot be controlled. Many years later, I had a brief conversation with Manfred Lopp, a great horseman and head of stallion performance testing in Germany. Manfred knew the German breeding system inside and out. I asked him about the tendency to breed more and more extravagant movers at the expense of disposition and correctness, and he looked at me and said, "The breeders need to ride their horses!" The implication was clear. He had some of the best riders working for him, and *they* were having trouble riding and training these horses! I think he was convinced that if the breeders had to ride the horses themselves, they would have selected for disposition, trainability, balance, or intelligence, rather than acrobatics.

The Power of Popularity

As the demands of competition increased, there began to be a specialization in Warmblood stallions. Some lines were more successful in dressage, others as jumpers, and within the dressage lines, some stallions became more influential, often more due to popularity than any objective criteria.

There were human equivalents to the power of popularity, as well. One example was Willi Schultheis, who came to epitomize the competition-driven German riding system. Schultheis was extremely influential, winning the German Dressage Derby himself eight times and coaching the German dressage team, as well as many successful competitive riders outside Germany. Perhaps no one embodied the German "driving seat" and German training system as much as Schultheis. The German driving seat could punishingly push into the back of the horse, making the horse hollow in the back and unable to swing his pelvis under the body. As successful as he was, it was Schultheis's seat that became a lightning rod for criticism of German dressage riding. What became known as the "German seat" was *not* a compliment at the time.

I had a film of Schultheis riding a gray horse through all the movements, up to and including Grand Prix. This was not a video pieced together from the internet (which didn't exist yet) or old footage, distributed in order to show a famous rider in an unflattering light. It was an official training video to be used as a good example of how the movements should look as they were executed by a master. I studied the video as if that was what was intended. However, the standout feature of the film was not the one intended, I am sure.

Schultheis's back and upper body were ramrod straight, but his legs were in front, and he was slightly chair-seated. Unfortunately, also clearly on the film, Schultheis's punishing seat and back drove down and into the back of the long-framed horse in an obvious attempt to increase engagement and impulsion. It had the opposite effect, which became painfully obvious in the piaffe and passage sequence where the horse was locked in his hips and unable to curl his hindquarters under his body. The game horse tried to answer his demanding rider with more energy, but with his back locked and hollow, his hind legs could not come under his mass to lighten the forehand. The only place they could go was spasmodically off to the side. It was sadly a failure at true classic collection as defined by hundreds of years of old masters' theory and practice.

Schultheis's competitive success meant that, rightly or wrongly, many riders tried to copy his seat; others were appalled by it. Regardless, when coupled with the long-backed horses required by the official breed standard, the result often became a dressage performance with exaggerated front-end movement and a disengaged hind end. For all the positives of the German system and the personal opportunities it presented to me, I had a front row seat to see what can happen when the forces of marketability take precedence over critical knowledge.

In the years that followed, up to the time of writing, it has become clearer and clearer that German dressage (which for all intents and purposes became the model for competitive dressage everywhere) decided a long time ago that the quality of rhythm was more important than collection. The list of horses that have been very successful in keeping time but could not "sit" is endless.

Around this time, I had the chance to take a couple lessons from Dr. Ursula Kinde, a veterinarian and dressage rider from Switzerland. She was visiting another veterinarian, whom I knew, in Pennsylvania. Dr. Kinde worked closely with Georg Wahl, who had been Chief Rider at the Spanish Riding School in Vienna, Austria, and then gone on to settle in Switzerland. He formed a famous partnership with Swiss Olympian Christine Stückelberger—they trained, among others, the famous Granat, a horse that became a European Champion, World Champion, and Olympic gold-medal winner.

In those brief lessons, I was shown firsthand some methodology that made me question the German system even more.

Another German

While I was training horses for the Daemens I wrote a series of articles about jumping for *Dressage and CT*, a magazine overseen by Ivan Bezugloff. It was a good magazine. Ivan was not afraid of controversy, and he featured a host of good writers and excellent educational articles, so I was happy to be published in it.

I hoped to expand my articles into a book, and I wanted someone to look over the manuscript. I had heard of a Dr. Henri van Schaik who had an impressive reputation. He was then exclusively teaching dressage in a little village in Vermont called Cavendish, but I knew he had won a silver medal in the 1936 Olympics on the Dutch jumping team. I sent him what I'd written.

I was competing a young stallion named Dacapo at an event in New England. I had still not heard back from van Schaik. I either didn't check who the judges were prior to the competition, or if I did, their names didn't sink in, because I clearly remember realizing at the event that he was going to be my judge for the dressage phase. I rode my test in front of him with double the pressure! At the end of my final halt and salute, he remained standing, and as I was riding out of the ring, he said to me in a loud voice, "I vant to talk to you sometime today." That was more nerve-wracking than any competition could ever be!

We did meet, he was very kind, and he arranged for me to come visit him in Vermont. We subsequently became friends for the rest of his life. He was a great mentor to me. Van Schaik came from a different era and kept in contact with many great horsemen and women all over Europe.

A Pivotal Film

Throughout his life, van Schaik was captivated by new mechanical innovations and gadgets. He had a computer early on, but for us who became his students, the most important of all was his video camera. He would take trips each year back to Europe, where he would film many great riders in little "home-movie" clips. Today, no rider in his right mind would allow you to film a training session for fear some small piece, taken out of context, would appear and ruin a career, but somehow the riders back then trusted him and let him do it. He used the clips to illustrate his teaching and his philosophical points.

There was one clip that stood out from all the rest. It was comprised of two short segments, showing Egon von Neindorff at his small school in Karlsruhe, Germany: one in the evening, with people watching from the doorways, and the other the next morning when he is all alone on the arena. He is riding an Iberian horse, Jaguar, in a series of movements: In the evening, there are some extensions out of a piaffe and trot that seem impossible in their power and scope. The next morning, there is a series of piaffe and passage. To this day, these are some of the most amazing piaffes I have ever seen—highly cadenced with extreme power, the horse teetering on the edge of a levade with great rhythm. All the while, von Neindorff sits in perfect form, quiet, motionless, balanced, as his horse's hind legs come deep under his body. It is the embodiment of the classical idea of collection, almost to an extreme.

Van Schaik used these clips like bait—just when you thought you knew something about dressage, he would show you a few moments that would completely open your mind or convince you to consider the classical route. When I first saw this film of von Neindorff, I was speechless. The hook was set. I wanted to watch it a hundred times—and since that time, I have. After van Schaik's death, I got a copy of this particular clip so I could use it like he did. When von Neindorff passed away, someone from his school contacted me, saying he had heard I had a copy of this film, which he had never seen, and was it possible to get a copy for his library? I did send it.

The Question of Motivations

Van Schaik, and particularly von Neindorff, upended the German paradigm in which I was immersed. Von Neindorff was one year younger than Willi Schultheis, so they were contemporaries, all their lives working with horses in Germany. Did they know each other? Why wouldn't the public make more of von Neindorff? It certainly could have helped diffuse the stereotypes about the German seat and German training, which were circulating in America. It wasn't lost on me that some of von Neindorff's most famous riding wasn't on horses of German breeding, but I was sure he would have explained that his riding school did not have a lot of money, and he often "made" school horses out of anything that was inexpensive, regardless of breed. Of course, this, in the end, was proof that the classical training system was universal, and also that a system cultivated by the forces of art would eventually surpass one directed by the forces of the market.

I heard a story that someone once wanted to show von Neindorff the high quality of young equestrians the German system was producing, so they brought him to Warendorf, to a barn where riders were assembled for coaching or testing. After three proficient riders, von Neindorff supposedly got up and left. His host followed him out, incredulous, asking, "What's the matter, Herr von Neindorff? Aren't they good?" Von Neindorff looked at him and said, "It's a shame they don't like horses."

When I heard this I wondered, was the riding I was doing, based on the German school of thought, yielding that same impression? Did people think I did not like horses? Was it unclear what my motivations were when I rode? More importantly, were my motivations clear to me? Was I going to try to make money? Did I want to become famous? Or was I going to try to make art?

I discussed these concerns with van Schaik many times. Toward the end of his life, when I would visit him in Vermont, it was the same routine each time: On one of the nights I was there, I would take him to dinner if he would pick a place. He would drive us in his Volvo Turbo, often on frozen roads, giving me heart failure. At these dinners, inside the formality of silver and candles, our conversations were unbounded. His accent would disappear in my ears, and his age would dissolve. It was often his wry wit, rapier sarcasm, his quick humor couched in his European formalism that made me laugh. It was fun to learn from him. By example, he showed me how exciting it was to keep learning, how I had to keep interested, exhilarated by and open to life.

Well before the science of expertise surfaced with Anders Ericsson's studies of "deliberate practice" that formed the basis for the "10,000-hour rule" featured in Malcolm Gladwell's bestselling book *Outliers* (I talk more about this in chapter 6).

I could tell van Schaik about my various explorations of subjects like martial arts and Zen Buddhism, and how they were informing my riding. He was always interested. It didn't matter if he didn't agree; he loved the conversation; he loved to challenge you.

I know it was the conversations at these dinners that were the inspiration for my first book *Riding Toward the Light*. It was also at one of these dinners that van Schaik offered to write an introduction for me so that I could go and study with von Neindorff. But after a decade in it, I knew the German system, and while I also knew that not all Germans were a part of it, I felt I had to move on. He had taught me too well.

2

THE 1980s:
THE PLANE
HEADS EAST

The Most Seductive System of Them All: Lightness

I WAS ON ANOTHER PLANE RIDE. I'd found a cheap red-eye flight from Montreal, Canada, to Lisbon, Portugal. It was different then when you flew: I was standing in line to check in, carrying a saddle. In front of me, a man was holding an Evinrude outboard boat motor. It was leaking oil and smelled of gas. Another man in line carried a rifle—no case, no lock. Apparently you could check in just about anything.

The flight was full of Portuguese fishermen. In the middle of the night, the whole plane suddenly erupted with the sound of unfolding tin foil. It was as if some sort of ritual meal had begun. I was already sick with the flu, and then came the overpowering stench of fish, which I can smell to this day. My stomach was churning like the air around the wings of the plane, high above the ocean.

Mystical Talk

It was January. From Lisbon I would travel to the little village of Avessada, where I had made arrangements to train with a Portuguese rider named Nuno Oliveira. Avessada was so small and the roads apparently so bad that I couldn't get a cab driver to take me all the way. He took me to Malveira, a slightly larger town nearby. I'd have to make arrangements to complete my journey from there.

I was already familiar with the French classicists of dressage, but I kept bumping into more current references to Nuno Oliveira. My ex-wife trained in Ireland at Burton Hall with Captain Ian Dudgeon, the Irish Olympian. While she was there, she met Sylvia Stanier, an impressive horsewoman who mentioned Nuno Oliveira (and would go on to, among other things, write a classic little book on longeing). Van Schaik himself was partly to blame for my curiosity because he'd shown me films of his friend Michel Henriquet, a French equestrian scholar and a student of René Bacharach, who in turn was a student of Étienne Beudant—both esteemed French classicists. Henriquet became a strong disciple of this man, Nuno Oliveira. And along the way, with the name, I heard all this mystical talk about "lightness."

I thought, I *have* to learn about this.

Who could possibly be against "lightness"? No sane rider was going to deliberately pursue "heaviness." If there was a tacit agreement among all schools of equitation that we wanted to ride the horse *lightly*, this idea of "lightness" being something to achieve seemed to indicate there were different ideas of what "lightness" constituted. Obviously, it was about more than weight.

Defining Lightness

Since there were no films of, say, French riding master François Baucher, whose work was known to have influenced Nuno

Oliveira, I had to go to the books, study illustrations, and read different accounts and descriptions to get a sense of who he was, how he rode, and if I could start to define "lightness"—his concept of it, his philosophy of it, and his system for achieving it. In my case, the philosophy of lightness took its lead from the classical masters: Xenophon (*The Art of Horsemanship*), Antoine de Pluvinel (*The Maneige Royal*), and François Robichon de la Guérinière (*The School of Horsemanship*). France had a long history of riders who were influential in the formation of the movements of dressage, the philosophy of lightness, and the limits of force. Listen to Pluvinel instructing the King of France: "The judicious horseman…trains the horse by means of sound judgment, patience, gentleness and tries to reach the mind of the horse." *Travailler la cervelle* ("work the brain"), as he puts it. A good horseman must never lose his patience and be harsh with a horse "for it is much more important to train him by using gentleness than by using force, for the horse who works with pleasure performs more gracefully than the one constrained by force."

So, the philosophy of lightness was one steeped in mindfulness. It was a partnership between rider and horse, turning away from domination and abuse.

The next question was, what were we training the horse to *do*? The French had a long history of using exercises that led to the supreme collection of the airs above the ground—the various jumps and lifts, and the ultimate lightness in the forehand with the horse eventually able to lift his front legs completely off the ground and balance on his hind legs. My concept of lightness and the training of the dressage horse took its lead from the same classical place: the horse should be trained to be able to shift his balance more toward the rear, lightening the forehand, which was by nature over-weighted, the front end usually carrying 55 percent of the horse's weight. The balancing and rebalancing must be maintained by considerable muscular effort, which increased the strength of the horse and contributed to his fitness and health. The process was no more or less than the definition of classic collection—the *raison d'être* of dressage.

What complicated the more current French equitation philosophy and particularly the idea of lightness was, first, the French Revolution. In a matter of a few short years the aristocracy was destroyed and classical dressage was associated too closely with the excesses of the elite. The trainers of Versailles were forced to flee, and so, the horses disappeared.

Second, a harsh schism was left in French equitation by the appearance of François Baucher and his rivalry with Comte Antoine D'Aure, who became chief trainer at the Cadre Noir in Saumur, some 50 years afterward.

In the competition between these two men, one sees the theater of the times, with D'Aure representing progressive forces of forward riding, outdoor riding, and straightness. Or, as Hilda Nelson, author of *François Baucher: The Man and His Method* describes, the historical and philosophical forces of romanticism. Baucher took on the role of classicist, his riding confined and reliant on dramatic movements. The amazing thing was, in this play, the actors were completely miscast. D'Aure came from the privileged class, the elite or noble type. Baucher was the common man who won the heart of the public through his standout performances in the *Cirque des Champs Elysees* of Paris; he had the political clout of a movie star, but not enough to win the commanding post at Saumur over D'Aure (the choice notoriously added fuel to the fire between them). To further complicate the picture, the circus in Paris was attended like the ballet of today: Baucher's audience was sophisticated, and he was a consummate showman, producing marvelous trick movements on horseback, and for these he was loved. His theories, as to his ideas of dressage, and his training methods, were a different matter.

It was surely an emotionally charged atmosphere replete with two massive personalities—so the "truth" as to whether Baucher or D'Aure was the more profound trainer probably lies somewhere in the middle. By looking at the source of controversy, maybe one can understand more about the concept of lightness, the legitimacy of its appeal, and whether it can be a reality.

Not an Angel

It is Baucher's theories and own words that are the most confusing; they eventually condemn him as a false prophet of lightness.

Baucher has by now been reinvented so many times by his followers that one might think he walked on air. Truthfully, he did not write very much himself, but there is enough to provide a more accurate picture than that painted by his acolytes. When one reads his own words, one doesn't get the sense that he was some angel on the horse. He wrote about complete submission from the horse, and the need to destroy any will to resist. He drove the horse from the legs and spurs so hard that his own legs had to be wrapped in bandages and the horse had bloody flanks. Then, he stopped any resistance or attempt to run through the bridle by inventing and incorporating severe flexions of the horse's jaw and neck. Baucher's own descriptions are compounded by the eye-witness accounts of a contemporary who actually saw him work and rode the horses he trained: Louis Seeger tells all in *Monsieur Baucher and His Art: A Serious Word with Germany's Riders*.

Considering Equilibrium

Perhaps the linchpin of Baucher's theory of how lightness occured was his understanding of *equilibrium*. According to Nelson's *François Baucher*, he talked about how "formal equitation defined equilibrium when a horse consistently went on his haunches, giving the impression that they are nailed to the ground and his forelegs raised considerably." He then explained *his* equilibrium: "This is a new way of paralyzing the total potential of the horse. Here the weight and the forces are equally distributed. By means of this just distribution the different positions, the different paces, and the equilibrium that belongs to them are obtained without effort on the part of man or horse." Two simple line diagrams in Nelson's book accompany these words. In one, a line rises up from the horse's croup to his head, referencing the imagery of rebalance common to classical dressage history. In the other, Baucher's system is illustrated: the line is straight from croup to head, parallel to the ground.

In her book *The Dynamic Horse*, Dr. Hilary Clayton defines *dynamic equilibrium* as a state of equilibrium in which all parts of the body move with the same constant velocity. An example would be a vaulter maintaining a stationary position on a cantering horse. During the dismount, however, the vaulter's body rotates into an appropriate landing position, so dynamic equilibrium no longer exists. In addition, she explains *stable* and *unstable equilibrium*: In *stable equilibrium*, a bridle hanging on a hook gets pushed, swings a few times, and stops where it was. In *unstable equilibrium*, a vaulter who is in equilibrium somehow loses her balance and falls off to the side, stopping farther away from her more stable position on the horse.

There are two more definitions that are important to any discussion of lightness: First, the *center of mass* "is a point at which the mass of the body is considered to be concentrated and around which the weight is equal on all sides." Dressage, in a way, is constantly adjusting the center of mass, and then trying to balance during the process. The word *balance* is used in equitation terminology to indicate that a horse performs movements and exercises easily and without any apparent difficulty in maintaining his equilibrium. A balanced horse going into levade shifts his center of mass considerably but still maintains his equilibrium through the process. In motion, the balance is more difficult than when standing, because as one of his feet moves up and down, faster or slower, the horse's base of support keeps changing. In fact, maintaining balance is a process of constantly losing balance and finding a new one. In general, the larger the base of support, the easier to maintain balance, while a levade, in contrast, has a small base of support, and so balance is difficult. The various exercises of classical dressage are intended to test that a rider has control over the process of balancing the horse, both over all four legs at regular paces and at rest, as well as the ability to progressively shift the balance more toward the hindquarters.

Contrary to Baucher's statement in Nelson's book, the old masters did not stay in one position of balance, "nailed to the ground," but shifted and adjusted. This "shaping" *is* the practice of dressage. I'm pretty sure Baucher was not talking about the scientific concept of equilibrium as Dr. Clayton describes it but a layman's balance. Nonetheless, he was confusing. When Baucher discouraged classical collection and said he invented something new, he *did*. He actually tried to redefine dressage by redefining collection, because he simply eliminated it. He encouraged the horse to balance farther to the front, giving the horse a larger base of support. Balancing the center of mass and finding equilibrium is much easier over four legs than over two. Even without video to watch, you can prove this was his goal from his stated requirements in different movements: For example, in the piaffe, the horse's front and hind legs should move up and down at equal heights—no loading of the haunches. Seeger described Baucher's horses as having no impulsion. Yet even if one added more energy to this frame, the hind legs might flex more, but they wouldn't come under the horse's body to carry more weight.

A great part of the difficulty of advanced dressage is this learning to balance more over the hind legs. One has to always keep in mind that the dressage process is not just about showing off some trick. Since the horse is naturally overweighted to the front, this training becomes an ethical way to help teach the horse's body to carry the weight of the rider without overburdening the front end and legs even more. Why this makes even more sense is because the horse's powerful hind end is quite capable of providing this relief for the front. So, classical dressage is not training something that is *un*natural for the horse—it is, in fact, all about developing something that is very natural. It's more a matter of *redefining* balance that is already there. Baucher felt the horse could be more like a spider, more equal in power and flexibility in all his legs, thus able to move in any direction, but the horse is not built that way. He has limits on the lateral displacement of limbs and has real differences in the power capabilities of the front versus rear ends.

Baucher's idea that dressage could still be achieved by letting the horse go more on the forehand would become central to understanding a "new school" of lightness, which diverged from the de la Guérinière (and others) idea of lightness. The latter is about lightness in the horse's front end developed from exercises to increase the strength of his hind end. The former emphasizes lightness in the bridle, which becomes much easier if you increase the severity of the bit or sensitivity to it, while allowing the horse to use his front legs to help carry the load.

Two Schools

There are interesting connections between more current (as opposed to the classical masters) Portuguese riders and equestrian scholars and French riders and equestrian scholars. One of the best books on French equitation, *Dressage in the French Tradition*, was actually written by a Portuguese rider: Dom Diogo de Bragança. And beyond what might be termed "historical associations" between the two countries, a new merger took place when France's Michel Henriquet—yes, the one Henri van Schaik introduced me to—met Portugal's Nuno Oliveira in 1959 and fell in love with his riding and training, became a disciple, and praised and promoted him. It was as if Henriquet had found a lost tribe in the Amazon, untainted by the modern world. Oliveira seemed to be a direct link to all that was good with French dressage when it was at its height, at least in Henriquet's eyes. There were others who were not so convinced. Oliveira, being the showman that he was, let his student run with the publicity. This part of the story I already knew when I arrived in Oliveira's stable in Avessada, and it was why I felt I needed to see it for myself.

There was only one other student at Oliveira's when I arrived. He was from Paris. He and João, Nuno's son, helped me find a room at a boarding house in town. It had a little heater and was near a small store where I could buy cheese and bread. I could walk to the riding school from my room. I was set. I liked João and came to respect him more as time went on. He was in a difficult position, often doing a lot of hard work and not getting much credit, but he was a constant observer of the circus that was his father's life. He knew the sycophants, and he knew who could ride. He lived under all the cult-like intrigue. If he had written a book about his life, that is one I would have loved to read.

Many years later, I was giving a lecture at an Iberian horse event and staying at a hotel near the venue. I was waiting to be picked up for dinner, and before my hosts came for me, I went down to the hotel bar for a drink. There, all alone, was João. I sat down next to him, and we had a nice talk about the new interest in Iberian horses, which was why we were both there. I told him I was a little suspicious because the people now infatuated with this type of horse didn't seem to care much about the quality of the animal, only that they now had a reason to buy the beautiful outfits traditionally worn by Portuguese and Spanish riders. He laughed, and I remember exactly what he said in his guttural, gravelly voice: "People love the folkloric."

Yes, João was eyewitness to the whole show, but I also knew he could ride.

The Drama of an Artist

In the beginning at Avessada, the rider from Paris and I had Oliveira's full attention in the lessons. Although Oliveira gave instructions in French, I caught on quickly. I think it was a solid week before he spoke to me directly, despite there only being two students.

Walking to the little riding school, situated on a steep hill, I could hear the opera music he blasted in the indoor from the road. He rode every single day in a sport jacket and a tie. He smoked constantly and carried himself like royalty. One could pass these things off as eccentricities, the drama of an artist. Frankly, it was a little difficult to get past his narcissistic personality. If a teenager played his music that loudly all day long, the police would show up! Oliveira behaved haughtily, seemed to have little empathy, and required admiration. He was legendary for his inability to handle criticism. Jean-Claude Racinet, a French proponent of riding in lightness, was once asked to write up a piece on Oliveira's book *Reflections on Equestrian Art*. Apparently, he wrote glowingly, acknowledging Oliveira as a genius, but made a small criticism, stating that Oliveira flippantly addressed one-tempi flying changes. According to a 1995 article in *Dressage and CT Magazine*, Racinet heard back rather quickly from a very close friend of Oliveira's, Jeanne Boisseau: "Your criticism about the tempi flying changes! The whole Oliveira clan is going to be furious. You see, I know them; for them, if you are 98 percent for Oliveira, you are an enemy."

I saw these traits first-hand, but I kept telling myself that I was not there to judge Oliveira; I was there to try to learn about lightness.

Falling in Love

Early on, there were certain striking differences in this Portuguese school of riding. One of the first things I noticed was the horses: They were amazing. In the stable, the school horses stood in tie stalls on concrete floors with only enough straw to slow urine. Others were in small box stalls, stallion next to stallion. They were tough horses, sound, and for the most part, docile. Watching them with the bullfighters, I saw horses with the fastest reflexes in the world. They were smaller than the German-bred horses I was riding back home, and close-coupled so they could naturally collect. They were beautiful, but I could also clearly understand that they were bred for certain utilitarian purposes for centuries: bullfighting or war.

The Iberian horse breeding program was almost the opposite of that of the Germans. Every horse was left a stallion; none were gelded! However, it would be a mistake to think breeders were not as serious or strict in terms of selection. If a stallion was rank in his behavior, he could be mysteriously absent the next day.

I fell in love with Iberian horses.

In the riding and training, again it seemed almost opposite to what I had been learning from the German training system. Very young horses were ridden in full bridles. One didn't encourage the horse to seek the contact; it was rather the opposite. When a horse leaned on the bit, he would be "broken off" the contact with flexions of the jaw or neck. This often produced horses that were flexed at the third vertebra, bending farther back in the neck and carrying their heads low instead of being flexed at the poll and keeping the poll at the highest point. The rein length was long and often looping, giving an impression of lightness of the hands. Of course, I had seen many Western riders who could ride on a looping rein if the action of the bit was severe enough. Lightness in the reins was easy to achieve, but lightness in the horse's front end was another matter. I knew I had to be careful not to put all the Iberian riders in the same box. I had already learned that from studying the Germans.

Style vs. Substance

The horses at Oliveira's were not ridden very forward. There was a lot of walking. I would later see this part of Oliveira's methodology, in particular, being copied incorrectly. Oliveira rode the walk with sharp spurs. He walked shoulder-in, haunches-in, half-pass. He turned this way and that. The result was that the horse became more and more sensitive to the leg and by the time he was done, the horse was on the aids and could be ready to even piaffe. He was almost *exciting* the horse with the walk, or *activating* him. So many people who copied him in this were achieving the opposite. In some ways they could not be blamed because Oliveira's message was confusing. There was always the romantic, poetic language: He would say things like, "No contraction," and yet muscles can only work through contractions.

He would allude to "grandiose music" or "the finest ballet"—the results to be obtained by "effortless riding," "supple riding." But after watching him ride for hundreds of hours, I found him to be, although tactful, very strong with his back and seat and weight aids, and he was not above disciplining a horse with a harsh hand or leg.

Oliveira's riding was disciplined, too, contained mostly in very small spaces. His arena was 15 meters by 45 meters with not a lot of room for forward riding. But his reputation was immense, and he used it, especially on his own turf. *He* could do certain things, but we had better not.

I remember once some girls from Belgium were riding at the school. They went shopping in Lisbon and returned to sit up in the viewing balcony and watch Oliveira work. On a break, he came up the stairs, saw the bags from their shopping, and asked them what they had bought. Reluctantly, they showed him a bitting rig, comprised of side-reins with a coupling to the crownpiece—a device to help set the horse's head carriage. Oliveira had a fit and lectured them about the use of such false aids, yet they got the idea to buy it from him, because he used the exact same rig in longeing some of his young horses.

There was often much language about what things can feel like *at the end* of training instead of during the process. There was a glossing over of fundamentals. Faults in position were overlooked: People copied Oliveira's forward-leaning head and casual legs. Sloppy leg position was allowed under the guise of softness, which Étienne Beudant called "riding in bedroom slippers." Flying changes were almost never straight. Too many people were captivated by the style, romance, and charisma and were steered away from a hard, analytical look at substance. Horses lacked impulsion and often carried their necks too low. Was this the influence of Baucher?

I knew it would take more study and time before this work began to make sense to me.

Truth in Pictures

In the end, I found Oliveira to be an anomaly. He was capable of producing bursts of true collection, but too often this was a result of a certain kind of horse he was riding, not the system he was practicing or one that could be replicated. It worked best for horses that already had very good natural balance. The more I studied this newer school of lightness, the more nagging a certain observation became. It was not the front end of the Iberian horses that either bothered or impressed me. The fault was in their hind ends and backs. I was troubled by how these horses, bred for collection, were often made to go hollow. I looked to the available literature and examined the photos from different representatives or proponents of this particular school of equitation. I considered hundreds of images, often pictures of the authors themselves or of those they thought were good examples of what they were trying to explain or demonstrate. I found in a great majority of these photographs that if you drew a line from the point of the horse's buttocks perpendicular to the ground, the hocks would be behind that line, pushed into the tail if it was hanging straight down. Even in clear attempts to show extra "sinking," when there was more flexion in the horse's joints, the hind limbs would not come more under the body. Any pictures of the airs above the ground would be pesades—high rears with one leg clearly cocked and unloaded, others with deep-set hocks but very hollow backs. None of the work that I could see approached that of Egon von Neindorff and Jaguar.

This school of dressage was missing something, namely the training of the lumbar and pelvic muscles—the *psoas* and *ilio-psoas*—to flex; it lacked a replicable exercise repertoire to build these muscles and then have the strength of the back and hind legs to pull the horse's front end up. There was endless leg-yielding, trainers forgetting that there is an inverse relationship between sideways movement and impulsion and power. All the side-passing was sending the horse's hind legs past his center of mass, effectively teaching the horse to *disengage* the hind end, not engage it. Exercises like the Spanish walk completely hollowed the back and forced the hind legs to take spasmodic, almost string-halting steps, again completely disengaged. There was too much infatuation with backward riding: too much reining back, even cantering and piaffing backward! Horses go backward when they are nervous and psychologically submissive, or if they feel trapped. To me, this especially was the antithesis of the great French horseman Alexis-François L'Hotte's teaching: "calm, forward, straight."

Too much of this kind of riding was contrary to good fundamental biomechanics and classic French literature, which could prepare the horse's hind end to rebalance his weight, and to me *this* explained all the hollowness.

I thought, There are too many good riders involved in this phenomenon to believe they can't see it!

I thought, There is something wrong with me!

But with more study, I became convinced that somehow all these riders deliberately changed their focus to the front end of the horse. It was as if Baucher's DNA had seeped into their riding.

Reins of Silk

By obsessing on the weight in the reins, "reins of silk," "riding with a string in the mouth instead of a bridle," no bridle at all, or using flexions to get the horse to drop the bit, these riders, like Baucher, had opened up the horse's base of support and encouraged him to put more weight back on his shoulders (rather than the hindquarters) by allowing a longer rein and often a lower neck. This changed the frame of the horse, putting his center of mass more toward the forehand, which in turn made it easier to balance him. I think riders became seduced by that feeling. It was easier, it seemed kinder, there was no sweating. It often used the increased ground reaction force (the force exerted by the ground on the body in contact with it) on the horse's front legs to display more "action" in the front, and this was "proof" that the horse was light. When one did this, one *could* get the horse lighter in the hands and lighter in the bridle, but he was not being prepared for the hard work of collection. He was not being made stronger, like a weightlifter developing the proper stance to lift more. He was not higher in the front.

Reactionary Riding

The more I studied, the more I could not see contact as a negative, nor could I see rein pressure as the definitive gauge for dressage.

Contact, or the weight in the reins, could be dependent on the personality of the horse. One might be very light in your hands, another might be heavier, depending on different levels of sensitivity. Regardless, contact was necessary as a measuring, diagnostic device to see if the goal of collection was being met. Many horses will bear down on the reins to block the rider's attempts at collection.

The real attention, to me, had to be focused on this question: Was the rider making the horse's front end light by virtue of athletic exercises that trained the horse to adjust his balance? Or was the rider just trying to make the horse "light in the bridle"? The latter could be accomplished just by using enough bit—the horse wouldn't touch it and he would be more comfortable with the ease of being just a touch on the forehand.

The danger of a school of dressage in which there is too much anthropomorphizing and too much attention paid to style is that the "romantic eye" will overlook some simple but difficult biomechanical challenges that may not be being met. For example, the French riders at the Cadre Noir in Saumur rode airs that were kicks of the hind legs. The lifts on the hind legs were straight-up rears with little flexion of the horse's hind joints. Much of the lightness in that school of riding was, again, just that little bit on the forehand; lengthening the base of support this way made things easier. The effortlessness, the lack of stress, of course was seductive.

It was as if this school of lightness—and I will be careful not to say it was the French school or Portuguese school because there were certainly classical riders in both who remained outside this phenomenon, and I was beginning to see that the most classically minded riders didn't belong to any one school but seemed to transcend national categories altogether—was trying to make a point to counter all the ideas of the current, popular, competitive German riding. I felt this "reactionary riding" had a huge cost: riders were abandoning a lot of the hard-won knowledge from Antoine de Pluvinel, Salomon de la Broue, François Robichon de La Guérinière.

When I left Avessada, the one thing I really knew was that there was one more place I had to go.

3

THE 1990s:
THE PLANE
HEADS EAST
AGAIN

The Spanish Riding School

I WAS RIDING IN THE OUTDOOR ARENA when my wife came out of the house, jogging toward me across the grass field. I stopped the exercise and rode over to her. She looked serious.

"Arthur Kottas is on the phone," she said.

What? I thought, The First Chief Rider of the Spanish Riding School is calling me?

"Here, I'll take the horse. Hurry up!" she urged.

The call was not completely out of the blue, but nearly. I knew I had to go to Vienna to see the Spanish Riding School and the training they used firsthand. It was the next logical step in my education. A year prior I had contacted Hungarian classical trainer Charles de Kunffy, whom I understood had known Arthur Kottas for a long time. Charles was kind enough to provide an introduction to Kottas, and I wrote him in Vienna, asking if I could come, observe the training, and maybe take a lesson or two. I had never heard back.

Now I was running back to my house to talk to him in person.

Kottas was very gracious. He apologized profusely, as apparently my letter had gotten lost in his communications. He had just found it and felt terrible about the delay. Yes, I would be welcome, but while he might be able to use his daughter's horse for a lesson, he just didn't have any other school horses available. He would arrange for me to stay in a pension within walking distance of the school. We set up dates, exchanged salutations, and I hung up. I was still in the kitchen, alone. I sat down in a chair. I was going to *the* Spanish Riding School as a guest of the First Chief Rider. I took a few breaths and let it sink in.

Like Classical Music

By then, I was a pretty good traveler. I had been routinely flying to teach clinics, but this trip made me more anxious than any I could remember. A lot was at stake. I knew the literature related to the Spanish Riding School inside and out, and it all made sense to me. I was using a great deal of their training system as a blueprint for my own work. But what if, when I saw it firsthand, there was a disconnect? What if when I saw it live, it turned out that I had misinterpreted it? What if it was different from the books and photos when I was there in person? Too late for second thoughts—I was on my way.

I would *not* be late, so I planned to arrive in Vienna early the day before I was to meet with Kottas. The plane connections all went smoothly. Kottas had arranged for a room, as he said, in a pension near the Spanish Riding School, nestled in the heart of the historic city, and after I settled in, I went out to wander. Vienna was beautiful in the fall, already cold enough to warrant a coat. The city looked palatial. I walked over to the school so I would know where to go the next day. It was headed toward evening, and the city glowed in a warm yellow light; the majestic buildings, the shops with perfect pastries, the whole place felt like classical music. It was imposing but somehow not martial.

That night I had a hard time sleeping. I thought I was coming down with something: I had cold sweats and chills like a fever. I called my wife, and she calmed me down. By morning I was fine—it was all nerves.

I knew I was to meet Kottas at an assigned time, but I hadn't thought about exactly where that would be, so, well ahead of the specified hour, I walked to the stables. From the barn, there stretched a small underpass, and the horses were literally led under it, across a small street into the indoor arena, which was on the other side. There, only a few feet from the street, were the famous doors that I had seen open in the films and photographs I had studied, allowing the horses and riders to enter the majestic school to the strains of Bizet, Mozart, and Chopin. There was no warm-up vestibule: one was on the street and then one was in the ring.

I was standing under the dark bridge, thinking about what to do, when Klaus Krzisch, a Chief Rider at the School (and one of my favorite riders), walked through the door. There he was, standing in front of me, alone, in complete uniform: brown tails and hat. He looked at me. I must have appeared lost.

Krzisch asked if he could help me. I explained that I was supposed to meet Herr Kottas but (clearly) I was not sure where. Krzisch just said, "Follow me," and we stepped into the school and marched under what I could see was the seating area, behind the wall of the ring's kickboards. We strode past giant pipes and electrical lines. We were in the ancient labyrinth where the nerves and veins of the School were hidden. We walked until we came to a beautiful office, which I could see was right off the main square of the town, logically positioned to welcome all visitors. Kottas was there, saw me with Krzisch, and knew the route we had taken to reach him. He was very poised, but I could see that his expression was aghast. He shook my hand, smiled, and said, "Next time, please come through the front door."

Corps de Ballet

We exchanged pleasantries, and Kottas took me to the Emperor's Box. Only a few other people were there; it was obvious that we were special guests. Throughout the morning, different riders visited the box and had a word with one guest or another.

It was like a dream. I could see everything perfectly in the arena before me, and it didn't take long for me to realize that everything I had read about the Spanish Riding School of Vienna was real. There was no disconnect: it was consistently the highest level of dressage I had ever seen, and yet it was in real life. Young horses acted out or clamored up the kickboards or bolted into the middle of the arena, yet no one got upset. It was as if the ritual, the tradition, the knowledge of the system was larger than any individual.

Early on, I saw horses with different personalities, and of course the riders had different personalities, yet the system was so strong that it produced a cohesive group. When the riders passed quickly, I could spy almost no difference in leg position, like a great *corps de ballet*. It would seem a soloist could appear from anywhere. The whole was greater than the sum of its parts. I think that is what the choreography of the quadrille was really about: controlling one's ego, not standing out, good or bad. Then, the group could produce something that rose above individual achievement. It seemed the opposite of competition where one person tried to win. Maybe it was something in the Viennese water, or in the choirs, and orchestras—even the people out, drinking in bars, doing things together. The artistic standard was high at the Spanish Riding School and so was the expectation.

The Human Side

For the next few days, I shadowed Kottas. After the morning sessions at the School, I drove with him out to his private stable and watched the training there. It was interesting to see in real time just how successfully the classical principles of the Spanish Riding School could "fit into modern clothes" and work with different breeds of horses and even competitive dressage. For Kottas, this transition didn't seem to be anything unusual at all; in fact, it was more the opposite. His attitude seemed to ask how a person could think he would be successful at dressage *without* a base in these classical principles.

Kottas had a reputation that he could be sharp when teaching, but I found none of that. He was gracious and treated me like a member of the family. We stopped at his mother's house on the way out of Vienna; I met his neighbor, and had cups of coffee at his house. In the evening, when the work was done, he made sure I had a train ticket and ride back to the city. One night, he and his wife and son and I had dinner and went bowling.

On my last day, there was an early Sunday performance at the School, and Kottas explained that he had to leave promptly afterward to teach a clinic, so he wouldn't be able to see me off. He suggested I stop by a small café across from the School for breakfast as the riders usually ate there before performances. I showed up and there they all were in civilian clothes, reading the paper, joking with one another. Kottas and I sat down and ate. One by one, the riders left until it was pretty much just he and I remaining. He seemed to let his guard down, telling me that his job was difficult, like coaching an important football team. He didn't have many friends.

"Next week," he said, "we have a riders' meeting. We're going on tour to England. I'm going to have to tell one of the riders that he can't go. It's not going to go over well."

Kottas and I finished up. I told him that he couldn't know how grateful I was to have had a chance to see the "human side" of his great institution, as well as the training system itself.

Art Came First

During the performance that day, I thought about what I had witnessed during my time at the Spanish Riding School. Philosophically, the German system was based on business, breeding programs, auctions, incentives for breeders. Competitions were places to prove the value of the product. Riders became salesmen for the "company." They promoted the product, took commissions, and received bonuses. What I had just watched at the School was practically the opposite. When I was there, the school horses were bred almost entirely for the School's own use. The riders didn't own them, and they were not for sale. There was no sales business to speak of. Art came first. It was performance art at a very high level; a piece of art laden with symbols.

What was its message? The riders wore hats that were relics of the past. Their coats were not the bright velvets and gold braid of the Portuguese bullfighters or the Cadre Noir, but a simple earthy brown. The whips they carried were branches of birch wood. There had been a careful, conscious effort to create an image that was not ostentatious, but humble; yet it was performed in an exquisite theater with brilliant chandeliers and a seating area reserved for royalty. In this there was irony. The riders performed in uniform, yet just when one felt it was a little too militaristic, a rider would reach behind his back to take a piece of sugar from the "sugar pocket" sewn permanently into his coat.

The performance, like elaborate theater, was a play in parts. It allowed the audience a time-lapse view of years of work, seeing the young horses at the beginning of their training make mistakes, followed by examples of their progression, finishing with the highest virtuosity in the airs above the ground, and the harmony of the grand quadrille, all accompanied by classical music. There were juxtapositions and links, recurring themes, and communion. It was a complex piece of art, concisely constructed to the finest detail, like a great ballet, novel, or symphony. It occurred to me it was perhaps the only form of art where a human being interacted directly with another species. Over the course of a couple of hours, it became a grand metaphor about the possibilities of man's communion with nature. It was not about dominance and submission as much as it was a story about the mutual benefits of cooperation and coexistence—and the possibility of inspiration, if one can move outside oneself.

Very simply, I felt what I was seeing was about the *art* of riding and not about the *business* of riding. I remembered a quote from Hans Handler's book, *The Spanish Riding School*, from when he was the Director in 1970: "Attendance increases from year to year, and gratifying as this is, we must take care to prevent the School from degenerating into a mere tourist attraction." If one mixes up the art and the business of selling the art, things might unravel. The wellspring of creation gets polluted. Motivations become suspect.

I had no idea at the time that disaster was on the horizon for the Spanish Riding School, precisely because the two *would* get mixed up. Due to a complicated series of political events and changes of directorship, the School has seen some radical shifts. It once seemed unthinkable that such an iconic place would alter. I think some would say it had already done its job documenting its system, sending qualified representatives out into the world.

It had already done all it could.

A Strong History

Technically, there are some key elements to understanding why the system at the Spanish Riding School was successful for so long. One certainly was the management of the human personnel, with a militaristic overarching structure. There were strict, well-known rules, which governed things like rider selection, the School's promotion, and behavior inside it, in spite of the (sometimes) large egos that went with the territory of elite performers. There was a strong history of mentorship. Younger riders would get nowhere in their careers without tutelage and nurturing from senior riders, especially since the bulk of the teaching was in the oral tradition. Written directions were mere suggestions to support the very specific knowledge and skills that any upcoming rider had to learn from a more experienced rider. Just by design—coats with built-in sugar pockets, modest whips—there was a conscious attempt to weave philosophy into the curriculum, with help and advice. In practice, a mere nod from one rider in the arena would get another rider, standing in the wings, to come out on foot with a long whip to help energize or engage a piaffe in its early stages. There was a sense that this was an elite community of riders, and the riders had to understand their privilege, as it could be taken away at times.

A Three-Tiered Program

The specific training program for the horses was, of course, what separated the School from other dressage systems. It was a three-tiered program. The horses were started on the longe line with side-reins. This introduction was so important it was entrusted to the most experienced riders. The work in side-reins reoccurred throughout the horse's training up to and including the airs above the ground. It had to be done correctly, since it would be an important thread in the program as the horse progressed.

Young horses spent the first year or so focusing on straight and forward riding. The next phase was the "Campaign School." Here the horses worked on collection, carrying more weight behind. Work in-hand was also used, evolving from the initial longeing. The trainer was close to the horse, controlling space and building strength for the ultimate collection of the "High School." Changes in tempo and balance and lateral work kept the horses supple. Like a great ballet program, the "dances" were made challenging to develop strength and elasticity.

Finally, came the High School: one-tempi flying changes, pirouettes, piaffe, and passage—all the movements of Grand Prix dressage and the airs above the ground. Depending on the temperament and ability of the horse, he might specialize in one air or another: pesade, levade, capriole, or courbette. The Spanish Riding School maintained the most historically accurate representations of the "jumps" that were loved and admired by the original masters. It was these jumps that set the riders of the School apart as the ultimate classicists and masters of collection.

And We Come Back to Collection

The whole understanding of the different schools of dressage, their pluses and minuses, their effectiveness or not, depends on one's knowledge of collection. People have tried to make collection debatable. In my opinion, it isn't. Collection is not an arguable concept subject to an individual's interpretation, as Baucher thought, any more than Newtonian laws of physics are debatable if you are trying to build a safe bridge on the planet Earth, where there are forces like gravity.

When the complete lightening of the horse's forehand becomes an ultimate goal, as in the levade, it governs the entire line of training. Straightness, impulsion, and lateral symmetry all take on an added seriousness. If the fundamental elements of training are flawed, at the very least a ceiling will be placed on performance. At the worst, it places the horse in danger of injury.

At the Spanish Riding School, I didn't just see horses that

could piaffe. I saw horses that could adjust the piaffe and change the balance more toward the rear until, on the rider's continued command, one front leg would come up and fold toward the body, and then the other. Sometimes, because it was so difficult, they would reach back down and touch the ground with a front foot to find balance and try again, until for a moment or two they were frozen in time in perfect balance on the smallest base of support. I saw horses collect with frightening energy, rock back and forth and leap almost straight up, landing back on the hind legs with mind-numbing strength and balance. And I saw them repeat this, four, five, six times. Throughout, the rider held excellent position, when the smallest misstep of the hind leg or loss of balance could have caused the horse to fall backward, ending in complete disaster. This was not cavalier risk-taking—the risk tested the skill and the skill controlled the risk. The goal was never to blindly increase the risk; the risk was a byproduct of plumbing the depths of skill.

The airs I saw at the Spanish Riding School were the best I had ever seen, and I realized they were a product of the best collection I had ever seen. It was the system of training there, always checked by the idea that this High School was the end result, which purified the practice. The obsession with perfect rider position could save a rider's life in a courbette. The obsession with straightness assured that as the difficulty of the exercises increased, the work would not inordinately stress the horse's body, risking injury. The obsession with impulsion would be a rider's doctoral thesis in the forces of energy. Every exercise at the School had a reason and purpose, and therefore, a proper execution. There were rules to follow and mentors to watch and copy. The goals were clear and could be explained and evaluated. The proof, in the end, of the greatness of the system was not in that it produced a once-in-a-lifetime horse or a rider that people could point to. Instead, it was a school that could replicate a superior performance, generation after generation, for 400 years. As long as the anatomy of horses and riders did not appreciably change, the system was valid and vibrant.

After my trip to Vienna, I was only more convinced of the modernity of classical dressage. Many of the images from that trip have never left my mind, and they have given my own system of training more structure, more understanding, and an even stronger foundation. In a small way, I was envious that I could not be one of the riders at the School. But, as I watched the glitterati of the international dressage world float, pushed by one breeze or another, I knew more importantly that I could *not* become one of *them*.

Dressage was making sense to me.

4

TODAY AND TOMORROW

*Are Competitive Dressage and
Classical Dressage Compatible?*

ALL MY LIFE, I have never been that interested in "winning." I saw early on that winning could be bought; it could be an empty ending if you somehow didn't live the process. After traveling so much to try to learn about dressage, a strange feeling began to come over me. I began to feel the different nationalistic schools of riding were becoming obsolete. The parochialism of the ones I had admired and learned so much from was choking them. With the advent of the internet, the information and knowledge base available to riders was expanding, but many of the schools seemed stuck, not learning from one another or the new science. My own journey therefore changed, and maybe it was happening all along, but the path now led much closer to home. There were still vast distances to cover, but they went inward.

People visiting my farm in Pennsylvania for lessons often bring horse magazines: They have a question about this article, what that person said, the frame of a particular horse. They leave the magazines behind, so they lie around the tack room. My interns know better than to try to talk to me about these articles. They know I will tell them to go to the library to study, to make sure they get their information from source material.

One day when I was puttering in the tack room, I picked up one of the national magazines and flipped through. I couldn't help but notice one article devoted to what young riders need to do to be successful in the industry. The piece was filled with advice like "master social media" and "treat every person you meet as a potential sponsor or donor." I found it very disheartening.

I remembered a quote from Alois Podhajsky's book *My Dancing White Horses*:

> The educational value of this sport will depend much more on the character of the person, and they will be greatly reduced if the proper attitude towards what is so often termed the noblest of all sports is affected by material considerations or moments of vanity. The idea of taking up a career with the intention of making as much money as possible out of it, and also the unhealthy quest for success for the satisfaction of personal vanity, have severely damaged the traditional value of riding as a means of developing character.

An Unsatisfying Answer

I couldn't count how many times I have, over the course of my training life, been asked whether classical dressage is compatible with competitive dressage. Why is this such a continuously uncomfortable question? There is nothing in the Fédération Equestre Internationale (FEI) or United States Dressage Federation (USDF) rules that would preclude a classically trained horse from competing, even competing successfully. In fact, there is really not much in the rules that is not essentially classically based—that is, the definitions of movements and even the selection of movements to be exhibited (for example, there is no Spanish Walk, there is no canter backward). So, the answer to the question (Is classical dressage compatible with competitive dressage?) should be, yes, it is.

Why, though, is this answer so unsatisfying?

I think Alois Podhajsky struggled with this same question throughout his life. He was the ultimate classicist, both as a rider at and Director of the Spanish Riding School, which—as I described in the last chapter—was a living museum of classical riding. He was also a motivated and successful dressage competitor, winning at the highest levels, including medaling at the Olympic Games. His book *The Art of Dressage* was a definitive critical look at competitive dressage, analyzing the biases in judging at every Olympics, from 1912 to 1972. Commenting on his personal experiences at the Berlin Olympics, he wrote,

> *After a long while, the results of the main dressage event was announced: "Kronos (Germany), first, 15 points; Absinth (Germany), second, 18; Nero (Austria), third, 19; Thersina (Sweden), fourth, 26," and so on. I also noticed all round me too a great deal of headshaking over this result, which was discussed everywhere, including the newspapers. The German judge was responsible for pushing me back into third place, because he not only put his own three countrymen first, second, and third, but placed me only seventh, unlike his four fellow judges, who had all put me somewhere in the first four. In a long article on the decision the German paper* St Georg *reckoned that I was entitled to third place even without the Austrian judge, who had placed me first.*

Talking of this disappointment, it is not without interest that many years later, in 1943, the influential secretary of the German judge announced openly during a lunch at the Jockey Club in Vienna that he had deliberately marked me down in the 1936 Olympics, being determined that a German rider should win. This meant marking up his countrymen and downgrading the dangerous favorites, and his tactics cost me at least the Silver Medal, if not the Gold, in Berlin.

These biases were so blatant that after the Stockholm Olympics in 1952 the International Olympic Committee nearly eliminated dressage from the Games. Only after a promise from His Royal Highness Prince Bernhard of the Netherlands and then President of the FEI that the system would be fixed was dressage allowed to remain an Olympic sport.

I think Podhajsky wanted to believe it was somehow possible that the ethics could overcome the politics, that dressage could be observed objectively and the subjectivity could be controlled. What Podhajsky did not have then, which we do now, were many studies on the psychology of bias and its real and often uncontrollable effects on fairness. On top of those forces, there are also social or societal pressures.

Two Numbers

If you want to understand competitive dressage, all you have to do is look at two numbers. One, the number of breeds of horses that are technically "allowed" to compete in dressage competition, and two, the number of breeds that are successful at the highest levels of competition. What you will find is effectively a very powerful monopoly at the elite level in competitive dressage, aside from some rare anomalies. (Iberian horses, relatively recently, have made a small presence on the world stage.) It is only the Warmblood, historically from Germany and Central Europe, which can succeed.

In 2010, a group of American scientists published the first statistical paper on dressage to be published in a peer-reviewed journal, the *Journal of Quantitative Analysis in Sports,* called "Scoring Variables and Judge Bias in United States Dressage Competitions." Over a nine-month period, 45,413 riders at recognized dressage shows in America were analyzed. One of the findings was that, on average, Warmblood horses scored 2.5 percentage points higher than other breeds. In light of other more significant variables in judging, it is easy to dismiss this advantage as relatively insignificant. However, if you know that in Las Vegas the house's edge in many games is a mere 3 percent and this is enough to ensure the casino will always win in the long run, then the 2.5-percent advantage becomes very significant.

One can ask the question, is it because Warmbloods are so much better at dressage, or has a bias been cultivated? From a statistical point of view, it is impossible to argue that there is no bias. Random chance alone would account for some horses of different breeding breaking into the higher ranks of the sport. Who would be the enforcers of this possible bias? The public does not really have any direct influence on the results of competition. It is the judges who select the winners, and winning is commercially important as a serious promotion of breeds—it includes publicity and free advertising, since most horse magazines report extensively about competitions and competitors. Remember Dr. Fritz Schilke's advice: No breed has ever died from lack of type; breeds die from lack of marketability.

Conflict of Interest?

The problem with dressage competitions is that many judges are also actively in the horse business. They teach lessons, court elite riders, train horses, buy and sell horses, and breed horses, which makes these judges extremely vulnerable to conflicts of interest. At least three high-ranking dressage judges in the United States breed or have bred and sold Warmblood horses. I'm not suggesting that there is mass corruption, but the design of the system lends itself, at every level, to influence, manipulation, and bias. In the same 2010 statistical analysis of over 45,000 dressage riders I just mentioned, the authors of the paper found, alarmingly, that there was a 10 to 13 percent variability among judges. To put this in perspective, you could ride the same exact test at two shows with two different judges and score as much as 13 percent lower at one show than the other.

The fact that one breed of horse (equestrian author Jane Kidd argues that the Warmblood is not a breed but a "breed population") has succeeded in such one-sided proportions seems like damaging evidence that this result is due to business rather than objective appraisals of riding. This is strongly supported by evidence, such as that recorded in Podhajsky's *The Art of Dressage*. In the United States, the *JQAS* paper reported that Warmbloods received 2.5 percent higher scores in dressage competition than other breeds. All of this demonstrates that dressage judging and competitions are not governed by an ideal standard but by a combination of political and economic pressures. To ignore the subjectivity built into the human mind is to ignore the findings of modern science.

The Goal of Homogeneity

The modern mantra of judges and of judges training—at least in the United States—has been to get the scores homogenous. When you have a homogenous sample of horses to choose from, it is much easier, but these more homogenous scores are also totally manufactured in judges' learning and teaching programs.

I have been involved in dressage competitions for 45 years, competing at all levels, and in administration of shows at all levels, from USDF-recognized shows to CDIs. While I have found great differences in the riding and the training of riders in the competition domain as a whole, the path to success at elite levels is fairly strict. It requires a homogenous horse. The rider has to cultivate a reputation bias. There is no such thing in dressage competition as a "dark horse" winning. There is virtually no chance of that happening. A rider must first improve her rank order bias. Later test times can be an advantage as studies have proved that scores go up as a competition goes on, and there are ways around random order selection. Knowing judges is important because judges are subject to peer pressure, like all people. Riders who take lessons or have bought horses or have positive relationships with judges will have an advantage. Riders must be seen by the judges fairly often, at prescribed shows, which have hierarchical value. Coaches and team representatives, acting like lobbyists, can get paid to help a rider navigate these waters. Their currency is ribbons and medals. No one gets ahead without them and their influence.

In the psychologist and researcher Anders Ericsson's book *Peak* he recounts a story on wine judging. A small California wine grower set up an experiment over a period of four years. Experts in the wine industry—sommeliers, winemakers, buyers—would taste 30 flights of wine in blind tests. The wine grower convinced the head judge to allow three of the samples to be the exact same wine. The results were, year to year, that very few experts judged the three wines the same, and often there were considerable discrepancies and opinions about the identical wines.

A False Ceiling

If we go back to the question of whether classical and competitive dressage are compatible, there are several key factors that shape the discussion. The first is, just as *The Principles of Riding* ended the repertoire of dressage before the airs above the ground, interestingly, so did competitive dressage. This is an arbitrary ceiling. Due to media coverage of competitive dressage, the public and most riders have now been trained to believe that the highest level of dressage is the competition test at Grand Prix. This false ceiling unfortunately directly conflicts with, at a minimum, 400 years of classical dressage literature. The sacrifice is a proper understanding of collection. Viewers and riders alike have little idea that the equestrian feat of say, a courbette of five to six jumps in the air, landing on the horse's hind legs alone, was in fact far more advanced than the Grand Prix requirements of piaffe and passage, or that the sublime balance of the levade was part of and proof of classical training. In the end, I think one could say that, at this moment in time, classical dressage and competitive dressage *coexist*, but if one accepts the definition of *compatible* to be "two things able to coexist or occur together without conflict," then they are *not* compatible. There is too much provable conflict.

One might get the impression that I am against the idea of competitive dressage. I am not. I simply believe horses and riders outside the accepted model should participate if they want to and be able to excel. They present the possibility of shifting or opening the paradigm of the "sport." The public would then have the opportunity to form its own impressions. To my mind, comparisons between breeds and types could only add to the overall public knowledge and appreciation of dressage and what it represents between horse and rider.

So far in this book, I have described prominent systems that are or were powerful influences on the evolution and perceptions of dressage. Another question arises: Is there a different system to which to subscribe? Or is there a new one emerging? If so, what might it look like?

5

A NEW
SCHOOL OF
MINDFULNESS

Mastering Not Medaling

WHEN WE WERE YOUNG, my siblings and I could get into some pretty vicious games. I can't remember how many times my father would head out into the yard to calm things down. We would always hear the same refrain: In exasperation, he'd shout, "Can't you kids do anything without keeping score? Just play the game for the fun of it!"

When you see certain trends in your personality repeat, you wonder how much of this was deep inside you, written in your own DNA, and how much was *trained* into you. The more I became involved in dressage, the more I came to understand what my father had been trying to say. My affinity for concepts of Zen Buddhism seemed to take more hold. Early in college, when I first became aware of Zen advice—maybe because of the way I was raised, maybe because of who I was—it resonated deeply with me. *Do a thing for the love of doing it.* It seemed to validate my natural curiosity and give me a reason not to be too concerned with approval.

Most countries will have similar axioms about competition, but American riders often grow up hearing or bearing the influence from quotes like, "Winning isn't everything, it's the only thing," from college football coach Red Saunders (often attributed to Vince Lombardi, the famous professional football coach), or "Americans love a winner and will not tolerate a loser," and "Americans play to win, all the time," from General George Patton. Parents teach their children that they can be anything that they want, and society starts them early, competing against each other to attain it.

What would dressage look like if its most powerful images did not involve riders standing on podiums with medals around their necks, endorsements looming, free saddles, free boots, fame and adoration from people who don't even know what kind of person they are admiring?

What if it was not about one person winning and the rest losing?

Your Best Self

What if dressage was instead about reaching a place where you are near the "best idea" of yourself? You might not be famous, but your horse likes and respects you, people like and respect you. You work hard, but you're not nervous about the outcome. How you feel about your work won't change much because of some judge's opinion. You are less concerned with how you measure up to an external yardstick because you are seriously engaged in how you meet standards established by *your own* tests. When you are riding, training, or teaching, you are so focused, you are often unaware of time. Even when a session is difficult, you feel right with your horse. The stiffness in your back seems to have disappeared. If you get frustrated, you can quickly recover your attention. Your emotions can't seem to get a foothold; the anxieties in your life seem suspended for a while. What you do together with your horse seems like cooperation: a mutually beneficial dance, and not like a continuing argument.

Have you ever seen pictures of people swimming in the ocean, their hands clasped around the dorsal fin of a dolphin as the dolphin carries them along? They feel excitement, fear, joy—their faces say it all. They can't put into words the rapture they are relishing, a suspension of any editorializing or sarcasm. It is a powerful jolt of pure experience, in that moment of communion with nature itself. Even though the positive effect of that connection can't be entirely explained, most people acknowledge it is important.

We ride horses. Do we find ourselves forgetting how ridiculously amazing that is?

The Negativity Bias

When I first started teaching riding, I quickly noticed that my students did not seem to hear any praise. All that seemed to register was criticism. When one rider told me that I seemed negative in my teaching, it bothered me. I decided I'd have to listen to my lessons and see how I could make them better. I started recording random sessions with students, and then later, by myself, I replayed them and simply counted the comments, making a check mark in either of two columns: positive or negative. To my surprise, I found that there were actually often more positive comments than negative and more praise than criticism. I knew I had to adjust my teaching style. What I didn't know was that I had run into a common psychological phenomenon, which scientists have only recently discovered. Human beings have a built-in *negativity bias*, and although the brain is remarkably plastic, it isn't altered easily, without effort. In the book *Thinking, Fast and Slow*, psychologist Daniel Kahneman explains how he and his research partner Amos Tversky found that people feel twice as miserable about losing something than they feel happy about gaining the same thing.

Why are we naturally anxious and negative? Dr. Ron Seigel, a world authority on mindfulness and meditation, explains in his lectures on "The Science of Mindfulness" that the brain did not evolve to be happy; it evolved to keep us alive and pass on our DNA. He talks about our descent from the earliest hominid, now called "Lucy," on the African savannah. The first humans were not particularly threatening. They were not very fast, nor were they big and powerful. They didn't have great horns or claws. However, they did have opposable thumbs and a thinking brain, one with the capacity to analyze the past and plan for the future. Our minds today can be anxious, fluttering, and prone to distractions because our ancestors evolved in a very stressful atmosphere. Constant threats of danger: from outside the pack, the never-ending vigilance against predators and natural disasters; inside the group, relentless jockeying for rank and rivalries for the rights of reproduction; and overarching everything, the regular reminders all around of human fragility and mortality.

The human life is full of unpredictable changes, up and down, and laden with a debilitating, anxious cloud. This is why for some 2,500 years, different cultures from all around the world have developed practices that give people relief from the mental stresses that can overpower them. These practices are in the form of meditations, of which there are many kinds—they are not all just "sitting on a cushion," but they *are* all about learning to control the wild horse that is the human mind.

The Task at Hand

In feudal Japan, the samurai were a warrior class. They were legendary for their skills in swordsmanship, with their lives continually at stake. The warriors sought any advantage to improve their skill, but in their physical training, there was always a ceiling. It was at that point that they became aware of the mental aspect of growing their abilities.

If there were masters of the mental side of skill-building, they were the Zen Buddhists. In some cases, a strange marriage of ideas came about for improving a capacity for physical violence with non-violent mental practices. The Zen masters were best at attention to the here and now, focusing completely on the present activity to control and sharpen the mind. "Chop wood, carry water"—that's it. Other things would take care of themselves. The point? We are at our best when focused on the task at hand. In a large creative study by researcher and author Matthew Killingsworth, it was found that the best predictor of how a person feels is her *attention to* what she is doing, not necessarily *what* she is doing. If she is completing a common, simple task but paying attention to it, she feels better than if she is doing something "special" but thinking about something else.

It became difficult to harm swordsmen whose attention was so refined that they not only left no openings for attack, they were psychically aware of your *intention* to attack. It was the Rinzai school of Zen that became famous for meditation steeped in action—or maybe making sure any action is steeped in meditation. For some fifty years, I have been trying to make this my horsemanship practice.

It is amazing how when a 1,000-pound horse starts misbehaving, it can galvanize your attention. Riding can become an astonishing meditation. You can try to figure out what it was about your upbringing that seems to always lead you to uncomfortable places or cause you to repeat mistakes. It could take years of analysis for you to reconfigure your responses and reactions to be more in control, more productive. Or, you can take up an active meditation like riding. Then, for at least one hour a day you are committed to *being present*—the power of the horse commands your attention. Your awareness is being trained, self-control demanded. Then, just maybe, this discipline can seep into the rest of your life when you step out of the stirrups. Working the horse and riding train your brain. You bring your mind back to the task at hand over and over. This control automatically leads to improvement.

There Are No "Big Moments"

Dr. Michael Gervais is a psychologist who works with many elite athletes, from big wave surfers to professional football players, including those from the multiple-Superbowl-winning Seattle Seahawks. In his podcast *Finding Mastery*, Dr. Gervais explains that, along with Pete Carroll (the head coach of the Seahawks), they don't talk about "winning" with the athletes. They try to develop strategies to help each individual be his best. When the players had clear philosophies, understood themselves, paid attention to rest and recovery, and practiced mindfulness, they excelled. The team focused on developing a culture devoted to these ideas, along with another important one: There are no "big moments," there are simply moments, which have equal importance.

There are no big moments because all moments are big.

In riding competition, we are very far behind progressive thinking like this. The relatively new science of the brain explains a lot of the problems with competitive dressage, but dressage organizations are very slow in accepting much of this science and restructuring the sport. Their leaders have very simplistic goals—to win medals—and constantly use phrases like, "We need podium riders." They measure success by medal counts, rewarding and ranking their own members with points and medal categories. They are trapped in a bottomless cycle of the endless solicitation of money, which is opaquely spent on the pursuit of more rewards for a very small elite group of riders and its goal of winning. When a country sends a rider to the Olympics six times, and unlike Michael Phelps, that rider has no chance of a gold medal, you are not witnessing a testament to one person's achievement, you are witnessing a very poor program of national development. The traditional culture of dressage, with its own goal of *mastery*, is hijacked by this podium mentality that is fueled by economic pressures of commercialism and destructive to individual development of both riders and horses—the tenets of dressage itself.

Your Practice Is About Improving

The natural risks inherent to riding a horse can galvanize one's attention, making it easier to focus on the here and now, but it is easy for that attention to get emotionally carried away by vanity, greed, fear, and other destructive impulses. *Mindfulness* is a direct strategy to stay in control of these compulsions.

Most introductions to mindfulness or meditation begin with simple breath exercises. Participants focus on their breath, in and out: an inhalation through the nose with attention to the sound of the air being drawn in, then a calm exhalation through the mouth, feeling the air depart from deep in the chest. If thoughts come into the mind, you simply let them go and recapture your attention to your breathing. Dr. Daniel Goleman, author of *Emotional Intelligence*, points out that the breathing is not the key part of the exercise—it is the *bringing of the mind back* that becomes the essence of mental training to pay attention to the task at hand. Your breath is a focal point to control the endless stream of distracting thoughts.

When riding becomes focused meditation, the rider's position is often such a focal point. It is no coincidence that positions of certain meditations and riding are very similar. Your seat, your legs, hands, posture, and in fact, each movement or exercise has built into it an increasing difficulty to test your focus and attention on your way to mastery. The value of the shoulder-in, then, lies in doing it as well as you can, and your practice is about improving the movement, and learning to know when it is wrong and why. It is not about winning a prize.

The role of the teacher or coach needs to be governed by

similar rules, with riders saying: "Tell me what I need to do in order to improve," not "Tell me where I need to do it, whom I need to do it in front of, with what kind of horse, so I can increase my chances of winning a prize." The rider has already won the prize! The prize is doing the shoulder-in! It is riding.

Going to competitions can be a good test to see if you are making your riding practice like the performance and your performance like the practice. As Ashley Merryman, an expert in the science of competition, states, the benefit of competition is not to win, it is to make improvement. How many riders actually use the scores of biased judges as their guide to whether they and their horses are improving? How useful is this strategy when we know that judges can have a 10- to 13-percent variability in their scores? Ask yourself how long you would keep using a car to go to work if at least once every two weeks it wouldn't start and you had to find another way to get to work. That's the kind of percentage we are talking about. It is serious.

Pure Experience

In riding, mindfulness takes on a double importance. For the human, mindfulness brings you closer to the person you were meant to be—your "best self." It develops a calmness with acceptance. When your attention is on the task at hand, and not on the endless scenarios of disaster or the fantasies of exaltation, which dilute pure experience, the event becomes more concentrated. Recent studies have shown that as much as 50 percent of the time, we are thinking about ourselves instead of what we are doing. The more attention you put on experience, the better you get at handling it—good or bad. This efficient and focused calm can help create a mutual focused calm in the horse.

The notion of competition being based on the pursuit of winning makes a person vulnerable to external definitions: you are an A rider, a B rider, a C rider. These categories conveniently let people who don't know you define you quickly, put you in a box, and allow you to do the same thing to others. People are complicated; too much external evaluation promotes anxiety and stress, especially if it conflicts with the individuals' feelings and ideas about themselves. These are debilitating effects, which can promote illness rather than well-being, eventually impacting the progress and health of the group.

Instead, consider the notion of competition built more on the idea of scaffolding, where an individual is important because the better she develops her own particular and individual skills, the more she contributes to the overall healthy development of the group. The group therefore has a vested interest in *all* members' continued development, as opposed to the group mining the highest skills of certain individuals for propaganda and then discarding them once a particular target is achieved.

Mastery in riding requires one to control one's emotions and develop attention (focus), which will in turn sharpen attention even more. Developing attention can help uncover your true motivations and give you skills to adjust them. It can increase your powers of perception, so you can edit information more efficiently; you actually see more, faster. In learning to focus, you discipline your attention, which leads to increased awareness, and that increased awareness will translate into better performance.

Three young Trakehner stallions in training in the Adirondacks. (I am on the right.) At that time, I don't think anyone could have predicted the sweep of the German breeds across America. Back then, in one weekend I rode these three, the Williames let me sit on the now legendary Abdullah, and Henry Shurink let me ride Romelos and Hexenmeister. I began to see that styles of riding were often dictated by the horses of a particular area and not the other way around. *Photo by Peter Grant*

A young Trakehner mare, Jataka, coming along. When the Germans brought over their ideas for stallion approvals and the 100-day testing, which included dressage, cross-country, and stadium-type jumping tests to appraise the horses, some of us were a good fit as riders/trainers because we were already doing this in the sport of eventing. *Photo by Mary Phelps (1984)*

Another German mare, Maid to Order. *Photo by Mary Phelps (1984)*

A German gelding, Lakotah. *Photo by Mary Phelps (1984)*

While eventing in New England on Dacapo, a stallion, I couldn't resist a wave when I saw a familiar face at the last fence. *Photo by Fritz Daemen*

In Portugal, hiking back to the village to get some lunch.
Photo by Judy Patrick

Nuno Oliveira and a rider from the Cadre Noir, Saumur, France.
Photo by Paul Belasik

On a steep slope near the village of Avessada lies Quinta Do Brejo, Nuno Oliveira's school and stables. To feel it, you must imagine the operas of Verdi emanating loudly from the long white building. You come in by rough dirt road; the impression is powerful, but it is even more powerful if you leave at night, on foot, until you can't hear the music anymore. You could hear it from where this picture was taken. *Photo by Judy Patrick*

My Thoroughbred, Mime, winning at FEI at the oldest dressage show in the United States, York Pennsylvania. *Photo by G.E. Perentisis*

A young Andalusian mare called Espera, being trained for Grand Prix. She was bred and started on my farm, and she is now owned by a friend of mine. To watch the potential develop from the very beginning and to be part of it is a magical experience. *Photo by Rose Caslar Belasik*

Practicing extensions with Espera. Even now, I am excited to go to work every day. I still worry that someone will find out how much I love my work and put a stop to it! *Photo by Rose Caslar Belasik*

6

THE ROAD
TO MASTERY

The Modern Study of Expertise

I HAVE NOTICED A NAGGING WEAKNESS that shows up in a lot of riders. They have an aversion to studying theory. They often have small chips on their shoulders when it comes to learning from books. They might leave a window open, just a crack, for studying very specific things about their craft—for example, they read articles on saddle-fitting but often stop short of books on the anatomy of the horse's back. They read about new and different techniques of riding in popular horse magazines but know nothing of the history that can give all the new and amazing claims of originality context. They will buy into methods that clearly lack any evidence that they work if the proponent is a charismatic salesman. What's worse is that these riders often go on to teach these things to their own students, compounding the glut of bad information in the horse world.

People often conjecture that these types of riders were attracted to horses and nature; they were never keen on school and education. They sought the company of horses because they never found a way to be with other people. This is nice pop psychology, but I think when you observe any individual seeking to master a skill or sport, you will find the person has the discipline to do *almost anything* to improve. The individual will consider obscure methods, but they had better lead to recognizable improvement.

If you want to supplant the *idea of winning* with the *idea of mastery*, the rider must take the personal responsibility to attempt to understand the science behind how someone *becomes* a master or an expert. As it stands, there is strong evidence that the person needs to follow a certain path.

The Teacher

I first heard of the work of Dr. Anders Ericsson, a Swedish psychologist, from another in the field, Henry "Hap" Davis, over twenty-five years ago. Hap, who has been a friend for a long time and does research in Calgary, has worked with many elite athletes, including the Calgary Flames hockey team when they won the Stanley Cup in 1989. Hap told me about Anders Ericsson's fascinating studies on how talent had far less to do with expertise than many people thought at the time. Ericsson was responsible for the 10,000-hour practice rule, which became even more famous as it appeared in articles and books like Malcolm Gladwell's *Outliers*. In its most simplistic analysis, the 10,000-hour rule simply stated that there seemed to be a fairly universal requirement for expertise across different domains. A person needed to practice—and practice a lot.

Deliberate Practice

Ericsson and others did not stop studying these ideas about learning skills, and today we benefit from an increasingly expanding *science of expertise.* I think it is fair to say Anders Ericsson has had to qualify the attractive over-simplification of the 10,000-hour rule over and over: it is not just 10,000 hours of *any* kind of practice—it has to be "deliberate practice." This is purposeful and systematic practice, requiring focused attention and executed with the goal of improving performance. In an important study with three groups of musicians (sort of a "good, better, best" range), no prodigies were found, and the difference between the three classes of musicians turned out to be hours of practice, with the best practicing "deliberately" the most. There were some interesting takeaways from the study. One consistent refrain from the musicians was that improvement was hard and they didn't necessarily enjoy the work they did to improve. (More details about Ericsson's work can be found in his book *Peak*, which he wrote along with Robert Pool.)

The concepts of deliberate practice apply very well to dressage riding. For one, deliberate practice is different from other kinds of practice because it has to occur in a domain or field that is already well developed. You have to be able to see clear differences between experts and novices, and it requires competition not so much in the sense of scores in a sporting event, which it can, but also in a comparative sense, using other performers or competitors as a gauge for your own evaluations—like with music, for example.

Classical dressage has a rich history of literature and artwork, drawings, paintings, sculptures, photographs and films, which document hundreds of years of continuous development of the art. The goals or objections are clearly stated and have remained relatively static, which has encouraged a steady, slow push to excel at a recognizable model or standard. It traditionally has not been a field that gets turned on its head every few years, leaving practitioners in confusion about what they should be trying to do (although lately, this does seem to be happening).

These models are what Ericsson might call "mental representations." An expert in piaffe might recognize or think of piaffe and be aware of lack of straightness, lack of engagement, false engagement, triangulation, loss of rhythm, all kinds of things, almost instantly. The novice will have none of this sophistication in a mental representation. The novice will need to learn about and recognize all these requirements in order to improve.

Historically, there have always been challenges to the classical dressage system. At the moment, we seem to be in one of those phases. If there is no agreement on what changes would improve the horse's performance, then it is very difficult, if not impossible, to develop effective training methods. If the current judges of competitive dressage or people in positions of power in the dressage world abandon the FEI rules on purity of paces or succumb to biases or don't study so that they understand the classical models and definitions, they will close the door on hundreds of years of long, slow, deliberate practice.

Good Teaching

The first requirement for attaining expertise is finding a good teacher. This can be difficult. Expert performers are not automatically good teachers.

I was once visiting a world famous rider's stable. Over the course of three days I observed him teaching a younger rider on the same Grand Prix horse. Each day the trainer rode the horse for a little while and then had the student mount and practice. Very quickly, the trainer began telling the student to lower his hands and drive the horse more forward. The result was the horse fell more and more on the forehand. The trainer became frustrated and asked to get back on the horse. He immediately raised his hands and began working the horse back uphill. The next day their lesson went exactly the same and everyone again grew frustrated. The third day was my last. I saw the rider in the viewing area before his lesson, and I felt I had to say something. I told him he might try to watch the trainer closely when he rode and then do what he *did*, not necessarily what he *said*. (I might have mentioned his hands.) In the third lesson, the same scenario began to play out: The trainer rode the horse, then the rider got on, and the trainer began the same refrain, "Lower your hands." This time the rider politely ignored him and actually picked his hands up higher as he rode the horse more forward. The change was obvious. The trainer blurted out, "There! There!" before finally, "You're getting it."

The point is, for a lot of reasons, expert performers may not be able to explain what they are doing, and in some cases actually pass on the wrong information.

Good riding teachers must constantly study the new science that might help them improve their students. They also have to be self-critical about their methods, to make sure they are accurate. (It is incredible how many so-called experts and teachers do not know which legs of the horse are doing the most work in certain exercises. Consequently, they use exercises that are contraindicative to their intentions.) They need to regularly upgrade their knowledge of biomechanics, physics, psychology, history.

I remember a story about the baseball player Ted Williams, who was known for his hitting. Williams taught others to hit, saying you watch the ball until it makes contact with the bat. It wasn't until years later that I believe Vic Braden, a legendary tennis coach, proved that you cannot physically see a ball traveling at such speed toward a racket or baseball bat. Your brain calculates the ball's arrival based on other information besides actual sight. The interesting part of the story is that when this new information was brought up to Ted Williams, he supposedly just shrugged and said, "I always thought I could." A student of a Ted Williams, realizing he cannot see the ball hit the bat, may feel inferior to his teacher. He may think he will now never be very good because he cannot accomplish this important skill (seeing the ball hit the bat), which apparently his teacher has.

Good teaching has to be able to point out mistakes, which, when corrected, show up in improved performance, and you have to then teach the student how to self-correct. Good teaching is not interested in maintaining the status quo. It must push the student out of comfort zones. It is not afraid of failure—it is in the failing that the brain and body recalculate a different approach or form, rejecting inadequate strategies, accepting and refining improved ones. When you consider this trial-and-error approach, it is imperative that a teacher understand the history of the field in order to not waste time on strategies that have already been proven unsuccessful. As I have said, classical dressage has a rich history of experiments and research. Good teachers of dressage will know this material.

Consistency or Consensus?

In good teaching, you must see consistency. Many people who are considered experts are not good teachers because they lack consistency. I have found in dressage that they lack consistency because they don't really understand the standard or the mental representations, or they can be talked out of it by surrounding circumstances.

I learned this lesson early. When I was in college, I composed a short story for a writing class. The teacher of the class, who was an up-and-coming novelist, loved the story and tried to talk me into submitting it to a contest. I told him I wasn't interested in contests, but he kept after me, and I gave in. One day after submissions had closed for the contest, in which he was one of the judges, he saw me in the hallway, stopped me, and grilled me on how I had changed my story. I was completely confused. I had not changed a single word of the story, but when he sat and considered it in the presence of his peers, his judgment changed.

In dressage judging today, especially at the highest levels, "blind" tests are unthinkable. Judges demand to see the label of the wine. They want to know as much as they can about horse-and-rider combinations. This leaves the process extremely vulnerable to bias. The competitors are then more subjectively compared to each other instead of being compared to a mental representation or standard, which is mutually agreed upon and clearly stated in the rules. The training programs for new judges concentrate on teaching prospective judges to be consistent with other judges, especially the highest-ranking judges, to bolster the illusion of a consensus. The problem is the consensus is not based on which competitor comes closest to representing a live exhibition of the rules.

Young judges should be trained to be experts in the rules. Instead they are expected to become experts at upholding the current politically determined hierarchy of style or consensus. If the judges did not know who the other judges at a show were, or what they thought, what would the scoring at dressage competitions look like? I'm certain the fear is that the scores would be all over the map, and this would only sow a complete lack of faith in any possible objectivity regarding judging and dressage in the minds of the public.

They Go Hand in Hand

When you train or perform in other disciplines and sports, simple measurements such as your horse jumping higher or your times falling (therefore you are getting faster) make gauging progress a little easier. In a field like dressage, there is a huge subjective element. Similarly to music, a clear understanding of historical objectives and standards is crucial. Good teaching, like good judging, should have integrity, which is not to be confused with stubbornness. Whenever possible, it needs to be based on recognizable or measurable qualities.

Riders looking to improve learn more and more sophisticated mental representations by trial and error and can see if they are getting better at accomplishing them.

Let's take the piaffe as an example, again. There is a long consistent history of the correct piaffe. The horse must "sit," his hind legs move less off the ground because they carry more weight, the balance shifts toward the rear, his hocks come more under his body, the forehand of the horse becomes lighter. The piaffe is proof of the collection process at the trot, with the horse almost at a standstill but maintaining a good rhythm. If a person judging, training, or teaching the piaffe does not note when the horse's hind legs have gone too far under him and his front legs have come back, causing "triangulation" (a fault), it is not a case of subjective opinion, it is a failure to recognize that biomechanically the hind legs are not able to carry weight so the front legs have slipped toward the rear to help sustain the load. This is a fault because it is the antithesis of the accepted mental representations of proper collection. Furthermore, and probably more importantly, the judge / teacher / trainer must not only know how to recognize a fault like this, but how to correct it. The strong argument dressage classicists make is that all the current movements have explainable requirements; when teaching or judging ignores or does not understand these requirements, it is not contributing to the overall progress in the field.

Built on Layers

A good dressage teacher must have experience through the expert levels. The main reason for this requirement is that dressage is carefully built on layers, and it is easy to let faults in fundamentals go unnoticed until they have created a ceiling that the rider doesn't notice until much later. Teachers who have been through the dressage levels themselves understand the sequence.

Consider that at the upper levels the passage and piaffe are important movements, demonstrating a high level of adjusting collection. Some young, talented horses have considerable suspension in the trot. Teachers and trainers who do not have sufficient experience can get infatuated with this suspension and encourage the horse to do it, even training the passage relatively early in the horse's career. This suspension can turn into a "false, hover trot": often a slow trot with suspension, but the suspension comes from stiff bouncing off the ground and not deeply flexed joints and powerful impulsion. If a horse has a hover trot with an inflexible and weak back, when later it comes time to train the piaffe, there will be issues: The piaffe requires the horse to "sit" or flex at the lumbosacral area with the *psoas* and *iliopsoas* muscles helping to round his back up and engage his hindquarters. But when a hover trot has been allowed to develop, the horse's back has become too hollow and stiff; when the rider asks for more engagement, the horse's back becomes even stiffer and blocks the haunches out. More pushing from the rider may actually only produce more hover.

There is ample information in many dressage training books explaining how and why to teach the piaffe to the horse before the passage, and this is one of the main reasons. If the horse doesn't learn to round his back and bring his hind legs under, as he would in simple trot-halt transitions and other exercises, he can be stopped from achieving a really good performance later in the final stages of training. Good teachers know these traps and pitfalls, and appreciate the necessary layering of training. They are always vigilant in their watch for slight faults early on, *before* those faults can sabotage later achievements.

Ego Control

Good teachers must provide good homework, and they cannot fall into the trap of promoting self-esteem instead of a rider or horse's performance. Many studies have shown there is little or no connection between self-esteem and performance. Good teachers will keep everyone's attention on the performance and be especially encouraging when there are even small improvements. Good teachers are very perceptive when it comes to small changes. It is important that they point them out to their students so the students get timely reinforcement, which eventually refines the student's own perceptions. Good teachers have to be honest in their appraisals of the horse's training and the student's learning. Improving self-esteem in the student is not the goal of a good teacher; improving the pair's performance is.

Good teachers control their own egos. They do not live vicariously through their students. Nor do they compete with their students to the point where they may consciously or unconsciously sabotage the student's development. Good teachers don't hold back information for job security. They build lessons so students are forced to face particular weaknesses. Rather than endlessly explain theory, they set up "puzzles," using choreography or tests where riders are able to clearly tell if they have accomplished new skills.

Let's say the left leg of the rider is weak or lacks control. The trainer will ask the student to do extra shoulder-ins on the left rein and maybe change to renvers, until the student and horse do the exercises consistently and progress can be measured, no matter how slow or irritating the process. Good teachers do not get bored fixing fundamentals. They constantly look for creative solutions; they do not ignore or gloss over problems. It is common for students to try to bully the teacher out of the hard work; the teacher has to stay in control without getting angry, but not relenting. The teacher and student and horse must become a team together as they challenge the next elusive skill.

When sports polls are taken in the United States to rank the best coaches of all time, invariably if not first on the list, one of the top choices is John Wooden, a longtime basketball coach for UCLA. Wooden began formulating his philosophy of coaching when he was a high-school English teacher and sports coach in the 1930s. Later, as basketball coach at UCLA, he went on to coach 10 national championship teams in 12 years, a record that still holds. He was the first person to be inducted into the Basketball Hall of Fame as both a player and a coach.

In spite of all the winning, Wooden's measure for success was the quality of effort to bring out your best. He said, "There is a higher standard than winning." Furthermore, he didn't really like the idea of coaching. He saw himself as a *teacher*. When you hear stories from students of his after their sports life was over, it is incredible how consistent their admiration of him is and how they all seem to talk about how far the lessons they learned from him—seemingly about basketball—helped inform their lives beyond sport.

In dressage coaching, in addition to the best teaching from humans, there is an almost mystical element of instruction that comes from working with a horse, a different species. There is essentially no verbal communication between the teaching horse and the learning rider, or the learning rider and the teaching horse. (In many other great experiments with animal communication, the human connects with the animal primarily through the voice.)

Part of what has kept me completely fascinated with dressage for such a long time is the incredibly sophisticated communication between two species *without* the use of traditional language. When you enter this world at birth, you really join the universe of nature and all the other species and living things that don't communicate with words. Lessons with a horse can become a kind of Rosetta Stone, allowing a person to begin to understand other communication and connections. Dressage is close to dance or music, where there are no words, which explains why watching one performance can make your cringe in physical pain or discomfort and watching another can fill you with joy and wonder.

John Wooden used to say, "Make every day a masterpiece."

The Student

There are only as many masters in one generation as there are masterful students in the previous generation.

Years ago I read an interview in *Shambala* magazine with a well-known Zen Kyudo (Japanese archery) teacher. At some point, the interviewer had asked something like, "So, you have been teaching in North America for a decade now. How's it going?" The teacher replied, "To be honest, not that well." The interviewer seemed taken aback and asked him what he meant. The teacher replied, "Well, I cannot seem to get these people to stop trying to hit the target." I think he went on to explain how goal-setting and ambition can get in the way of mastering technique, and understanding the process is what is important. Finally the concerned interviewer asked, "What are you going to do next? Are you going back to Japan?" To which the teacher answered, quite seriously, "Oh, no. It has become my practice to find out why this is bothering me so much!"

Let's say you take up any activity and at first it is not too difficult. You receive some praise, and that reward carries you through another round of practice. In any activity, the progress will soon slow down. At the highest levels of performance, months of hard practice may yield a minute of improvement in the time of a runner. A musician may practice months and months to play one difficult piece of music. The time for a rider between when she learns to strike off on the left or right lead and when she can execute tempi changes may be years.

When your motivation is based on external rewards, it is doubtful that you will stick it out through 10,000 hours of practice, much less 10,000 hours of *deliberate practice* (as we discussed in the previous chapter), many of which will be hours outside your comfort zone. The rewards will be too few and too far between to sustain such effort. To become an expert at anything, a person has to find some intrinsic rewards, a love of a particular craft, a driving curiosity, but almost always, quite simply, a desire to do it *well*. This determination surpasses the effort involved. The best at anything are not sustained by prizes; they are sustained by the consuming drive to *get better*. They never seem satisfied to continuously repeat strategies of the past. Improvement is hard, and experts don't necessarily enjoy the work they do to achieve it.

Strategies for Success

Having said that, there are strategies that can make studying and learning easier, with a higher percentage of success. People will gain weight over a period of many years, but one day make a decision to try to lose weight and do it in a period of months or weeks. You can make the *decision* to lose weight in one day, but you cannot lose the weight in one day. They are different. If you aim to lose one pound a week, in one year you have the potential to lose 50 pounds! Plus, you give yourself a chance to adjust to a new lifestyle of nutrition and exercise, slowly. When you set targets that are too ambitious or unrealistic, you can poison the well of motivation, and in the end, accomplish almost nothing.

Some Zen masters were so tired of archery students trying to hit the target instead of working on their form that they moved the target until it was only a couple of feet from the archers so that the archers couldn't miss it. Then the archers forgot about trying to hit the target and concentrated on form.

Practice is cumulative. Science shows us it is many little steps toward expertise. Nurture the beginner's mind. As they say in Zen, in the mind of the expert, few things are possible; in the mind of the beginner, *all* things are possible. Stay curious.

In riding, we have an old term we use in the training of horses that almost all horsemen know: it is "overfacing." Good trainers know if you ask a young, game horse to jump too high or run too fast too early, the horse might just suddenly, often dramatically, quit. No amount of incentive, positive or negative, will convince the horse to try again. It is as if there is a mechanical or psychological spring that can be overloaded, and if it is, it is not repairable. In practice, you can overface yourself or others can do it to you. You must learn to train outside your comfort zone, but you must also allow time for recovery and reflection.

In good training, the process can be made to be more enjoyable. One of the most successful groups of riders I work with has made competitions a social event. They go out and eat good food, stay at a nice hotel, and enjoy the camaraderie of seeing each other, in spite of their busy professional and family schedules. They support each other through the ups and downs of performances. Every rider in the group has substantially improved over the years. It is like how in the 1950s in Paris there was a vibrant artistic community. Many of the artists knew each other. They socialized at the same restaurants and bars. Their competitiveness and awareness of each other's work inspired them. I remember Henri van Schaik talking about competing at the world-class level, and when he won the silver medal at the Olympics in 1936. He said about his fellow riders, "Paul, we were all friends. We would all go out to dinner together after the shows. No one wanted to win because whoever won had to buy the wine!"

Hard Bark

Remember that small changes improve performance. You will need full attention to become aware of them; this is where mindfulness becomes so important. Monitor yourself, spot mistakes. When watching video of yourself riding, try to learn to be fair. Once in a while, compare it to the year before. If you have been training correctly, you will see big differences. Learn to know for yourself whether or not you have improved.

See if you can view performances more objectively, even your own. Practice comparing: understand the classical standards and see if you can articulate why one performance meets them better than another. Critical thinking is not mean, and remember, it is based more on performance than on self-esteem. It can sting; life is not nice. Students need to build up a little hard bark over time, to protect themselves, but also to prevent cynicism. Is the received criticism valid, even if it comes in a distasteful presentation? That is not to say you should accept disrespect or critique delivered in an abusive form. Today all professionals and competitors associated with the United States Equestrian Federation (which is a required membership to compete at recognized shows) must complete "Safe Sport" training. We should all be able to recognize trouble spots and establish appropriate boundaries in teaching and coaching.

One of the benefits of difficult training—becoming an expert rider—should be developing willpower and the ability to control impulses, which will make you a better person. When you hear criticism, divorce the words from the person being critical of you, and look at what is being said like words written on a page with no tone of voice. As you learn to be your own best critic, also learn to see if criticism from others has merit. Do not reflexively dismiss it if it disagrees with your own mental construction. If when you analyze criticism you can't tell if it is valid, ask someone else for an additional opinion.

Community

There was a time when my stable was in a remote part of the country, the Adirondack Mountains of New York. It was beautiful place to live, and it afforded me time to really practice—hours without interruption to explore and hone my skills. But, I felt increasingly cut off from the horse culture I was so familiar with, and eventually I chose to move back toward the heart of horse country and horse people, in Pennsylvania. I knew very well what this country was like because my first full-time job with horses after graduating from college was working for George "Frolic" Weymouth in Chadds Ford, Pennsylvania. Tom Donehauer, a friend of mine from college, was driving horses for Frolic and needed some help on the job. Frolic, an artist and conservationist, was opening the beautiful Brandywine Museum of Art, converted from an old mill on the banks of the Brandywine River and devoted to the paintings of the Brandywine Valley: Howard Pyle, N.C. Wyeth, Andrew Wyeth.

Frolic was a descendant of the Du Ponts, a graduate of Yale, and a gifted painter in his own right. He had a bucolic, pristine farm called The Big Bend, situated on the edge of the Brandywine River. He went on to be instrumental in forming the Brandywine Conservancy to help preserve some of the most beautiful horse country in the United States.

If you read Frolic's biography and achievements, you could very easily miss the real Frolic. He loved to entertain with his carriaging and was an incredible whip. I saw him do things driving four horses that I would have thought impossible. People wanted him to be on the equestrian team, but Frolic would have none of it. It had to be fun. There had been enough structure in his life. He loved to poke holes in pomposity and was one of the least judgmental people I have ever met. I have never met anyone who got as much joy out of life as Frolic, and those of us who worked for him in those days all got the lesson: If you are not enjoying what you are doing, you might want to rethink why you are doing it. It was there in southern Pennsylvania where I began to see the depth of the horse community and the importance of any horse community to an individual horseman.

Within a 50-mile radius of the area where my stable was in Pennsylvania, there were a hundred riders who were on various equestrian teams: professional jumpers, eventers, dressage riders, and driving enthusiasts. There was foxhunting and racing—it was country rich in horses and equine experts. If you had made a circle with a 50-mile radius around my farm in the Adirondack Mountains of New York, you would find within only a few horses. Dr. Henri van Schaik would say his eye would deteriorate if he did not go to Europe every so often to see very good riding. I came to realize what he meant; it was really the lack of community. I eventually had to return to horse country and the community there.

I became more involved in the business of dressage competitions and horse shows. I served on various committees of different dressage organizations. I eventually was president of one of the most distinguished dressage and combined training organizations in the United States, which annually ran the international CDI Dressage at Devon, and the international CCI three-day event Chesterland (which became Fair Hill). In these activities, it was inevitable that one became embroiled in politics. The volunteers who administered the events were amazing people, but I could not hide from the destructive mindset prevalent among certain competitors and organizers who obsessed over scores.

I saw the synergy of community was powerful. In all the mutual interest, support, and comparison, there could be a continuous elevation of the quality of dressage. I also saw that the same community could be dark, materialistic, incestuous, jealous, destructive, competitive, petty.

As time went on, I grew tired of the rivalries, the defensive protectionism, the competing parochial materialism inherent in competitive dressage. These ways of thinking have had a long run in and around the dressage arena. They have not produced collegiality or a collective increase in skill or knowledge. They have produced roadblocks, made learning difficult, and treated critical thought as disloyalty to a particular school. They have encouraged rampant drug abuse with horses and produced powerful national and international organizations that have turned a blind eye toward other abusive practices that impact both young people and young horses.

I also found myself at odds with a group of dressage promoters who felt that dressage needed to have a wider audience.

Like Fly-Fishing

A popular topic of discussion in the dressage world is that the sport needs more people to see and appreciate it. Bigger prizes are promoted, and competitions are held at venues that hold more spectators where the event becomes an entertainment exhibition based on the most popular sports, such as the football model—an activity produced to develop massive audience appeal.

But what if those leading competitive dressage in this direction have the metrics all wrong?

Take fly-fishing for an example. A combination of art and sport, similar to dressage, fly-fishing has grown tremendously, and it is a big, successful business. But fly-fishermen don't spend their money on tickets to go to Las Vegas and watch specialists fish. They buy equipment and take lessons; they pay for guides to take them on trips so they can fish themselves. Their goal is to get away from the competitive stresses of their lives to have a personal experience with nature. It is a type of meditation. When they win a prize of a beautiful fish, what do they do? They throw it back in the water. Fly-fishing is the embodiment of process. It is all about *the fishing*, not catching the prize.

Fly-fishing is also a business, but it is not about getting more people to watch, it is about getting more people to do it. This mentality used to be and should still be the essence of dressage riding.

As fly-fishing promotes this mentality, there are many positive secondary benefits. In the wake of this growth, participants become advocates for clean water and are more ecologically conscious, with far-reaching benefits outside the seemingly simplistic domain. If those who promote the sport of dressage don't understand that the real appeal of dressage is the individual experience of doing it, not the social experience of watching it, they can actually harm the art by missing the importance of the specifics of the mental representations. The models that are used to gauge its quality can get watered down or misunderstood, or in some cases politically sabotaged for all kinds of personal reasons.

People will always want to make money off any endeavor. They form their own descriptions of what the activity is, and in the worst cases, the descriptions become more powerful than the original action or endeavor. Business shapes the consciousness of customers and followers. One day, people might wonder, where did the authentic riders and trainers go? It could become impossible to tell who is performing the art, or what real dressage even looks like.

My ideas about competition evolved over time. And the comparisons with my fellow horsemen and women need not always be judgmental. They could serve to inspire. They could be an impetus to improve. My life and travels formed a large laboratory in which to watch failures and successes, good riding and bad. Inside a culture of so many good horsemen and women, many who truly loved horses and the life around them, I had to find my own way. If I copied someone else, it would be obvious to all the experts, and it meant that even at my very best I would only be a second-rate imitation. Physical development of the craft was part of the journey, and there were good teachers and examples available to guide me on this path, but to become a really good horseman, I needed to study the literature, science, and theory.

In my horse community in Pennsylvania, philanthropic, forward-thinking horse people took care of this need. I could study in the Jean Austin du Pont library on the veterinary school campus of the University of Pennsylvania at New Bolton Center. The library was devoted to scientific equine studies and papers, but also housed an amazing collection of historical books on horsemanship donated by the wealthy Philadelphia horseman Fairman

Rogers. Books by the Duke of Newcastle, François Robichon de La Guérinière, Salomon de La Broue—they were all there. I could go in and study as long as I wanted to, for free. The educational resources were outstanding. Van Schaik had a nice library for an individual, but the Fairman Rogers collection was one of the best in the world.

There was a physical aspect to mastering the craft of horsemanship, but there was also an educational, theoretical development necessary. And you couldn't find this just anyplace. (I feel that remains the case, even now with the internet.) Finally, one needed to gain an understanding of the ethical development of the relationship between humans, horses, and nature.

Living for the Process

Of course, in an area such as where I was in Pennsylvania, there were big egos, but there were also very humble horse people, rich and poor, who had a religious respect for the horse and the life around them. Some, like Frolic Weymouth, gave their farms over to conservancies so the land would remain undeveloped. The care of the horse was, by itself, an art form. There were individuals with such awareness that they could walk into a stable of 15 horses in the dark and know if one of the horses was not feeling right. Their mindfulness and ability to focus attention was almost telepathic. It was not uncommon to see a woman dressed up beautifully for a party stepping out of a barn, picking bits of hay off her dress because she had to do night check before she left for the evening.

The sophisticated and varied community was daunting, but

it was supportive of developing our particular passion: On their days off, people would often go to watch some other horse discipline. World-caliber horse activities were put on by staffs of hundreds of unpaid volunteers. If you forgot a piece of equipment at a horse event, you could borrow it from the world champion who was parked next to you. While many of the horsemen and women had the resources to buy winning horses in any discipline, what really moved them was if they developed something special with a horse they bred or raised. They placed the highest value on *process*—in fact they lived for the process and not only the outcome. Winning the wrong way was distasteful.

In all this mutual interest and support, there can be a mutual elevation of purpose. A student's curiosity and grit can be the clay sculpted by a generous teacher, who is recognized by a forward-thinking society, which shows it values this kind of development by promoting a culture that encourages that student's curiosity and grit. This can be a way to live with and train horses that stands out like a Zen painting, a simple circle brushed onto a clean white paper. There is no end to the cycle.

EPILOGUE

THE
DESTINATION

The Path Is Not an Itinerary

THERE IS AN OLD ZEN STORY about destinations. It goes something like this. A student comes up to the master and asks, "If I practice diligently, how long might it take before I become a master?" The master begrudgingly answers, "Maybe 20 years." The student winces and says, "What if I practice especially hard?" The master replies, "Then 30 years." The student, now perplexed, asks, "What if I practice harder than all the other students?" "That will be 40 years!" says the master. Completely confused, the student queries, "Why is it that every time I say I will work harder, the time to reach mastery gets longer?" And the master answers, "With one eye on the destination, you have only one eye on the practice."

How long will it be before people will not flinch when they hear words like "path" and "meditation"? How much more science will there need to be before the old paradigm that winning is everything begins to weaken?

A path is like the history of the evolution of a successful species. If you look backward, the progression seems so orderly, logical, as if it were guided by an omniscient being. The end seems inevitable. Yet, we know hundreds of choices in the natural selection were failures and dead ends that have disappeared. We know that the process is not a movement toward any goal but instead a process of constantly moving away from more immediate forces and pressures.

Young people are told to want to be a lawyer or a doctor or to go to the Olympics. They pick a destination and work backward from it. The goal informs and governs their choices. If a person does reach the destination this way, like the history of a successful species, that process seems orderly, as if the destination were inevitable, a logical result of hard work. Other people might see this as proof of the usefulness of such a plan of apparent discipline. They can conveniently ignore all the valiant efforts in life that end in failure. How many people never reach projected, fanciful destinations, or if they do, they feel empty and wish they had changed course?

One has to be careful. All these itineraries are projections into a future we cannot know. Just as evolution is a historical account of what really happened, a path is a historical account of what really happened, not what you wanted to happen or thought would happen. A path can be unsatisfying if it doesn't follow a fantasy, it can be frustrating because it can be out of your control. Disease, natural disasters, any constellation of events beyond our control can interrupt any itinerary. The one thing you *can* control with practice, lots of *deliberate practice*, is the way you respond to life. If success is described mostly by whether you win or not, whether you hit the target, life can begin to be defined by outward visible achievement. The problem is—and we are especially seeing it today—that if that outward achievement is acquired by epidemic cheating, or by sheer random luck, or by buying it if you have enough power and money, then it can cover up a complete lack of *inner* achievement. Many times the only person who is really going to know is you. Being advised to not aim for the target is not to say you shouldn't try to hit the target or just accept incompetence. No—it's just a constant reminder that hitting the target with the wrong attitude is meaningless. Go ahead, practice hard, aim for the target, but do it the right way, and don't forget or be talked out of maintaining a balance of the inner and outer self.

A master is not necessarily someone who is an expert at a craft. It is possible expertise can come fairly early on in life to someone, and that person stops growing at that point. The individual is satisfied, convinced. He or she repeats the success, believing he or she has acceptable mastery.

The biggest mistake of all is to *think* you have hit the target.

A master is someone who evolves, who knows about randomicity, who understands luck, who shies away from judgment—someone who can adapt. Someone who keeps on living; someone who never stops trying to improve.

Recommended Reading List

Altered Traits
by Daniel Goleman and Richard J. Davidson

Advanced Techniques of Riding
by the German National Equestrian Federation

Dressage in the French Tradition
by Dom Diogo de Bragança

The Dynamic Horse
by Hilary M. Clayton

The Complete Training of Horse and Rider
by Alois Podhajsky

François Baucher: The Man and His Method
by Hilda Nelson

The Gymnasium of the Horse
by Gustav Steinbrecht

Peak
by Anders Ericsson and Robert Pool

The Spanish Riding School
by Hans Handler

Zen and Japanese Culture
by D.T. Suzuki

References

Dias, Ana, Johnston, Mary S., Lucitti, Jennifer, Moran, Katy, M. Neckameyer, Wendy S. "Scoring Variables and Judge Bias in United States Dressage Competitions." *Journal of Quantitative Analysis in Sports*, Vol. 6. Issue 3 (2010):13-13.Print.

Ericsson, Anders and Pool, Robert. *Peak: Secrets from the New Science of Expertise*. New York: Houghton Mifflin, 2016.

Gervais, Michael. "Finding Mastery. Micheal Gervais and Pete Carroll Talk Sports Psychology." Findingmastery.net, July 7, 2015.

Kahneman, Daniel. *Thinking, Fast and Slow*. New York: Farrar, Strauss and Giraux, 2011.

Nelson, Hilda. *Francois Baucher: The Man and His Method*. London: J.A. Allen, 1992.

Podhajsky, Alois. *The Art of Dressage*. New York: Doubleday and Co., 1976.

      ---. *My Dancing White Horses*. New York: Holt, Rinehart and Winston, 1965.

Seeger, Louis. *Monsieur Baucher and His Art: A Serious Word with Germany's Riders*. Translated by Cynthia Hodges. Edmonds: Auriga Books, 2010.

Seigel, Ron. "The Science of Mindfulness: Working With Anxiety, Depression, and Other Everyday Problems." Youtube.com, August 25, 2016. 1:05:49.

Index